Up All Night

Up All Night

Martha Gies

Oregon State University Press
Corvallis

The paper in this book meets the guidelines for permanence and
durability of the Committee on Production Guidelines for Book Longevity
of the Council on Library Resources and the minimum requirements of
the American National Standard for Permanence of Paper for Printed
Library Materials Z39.48-1984.

Library of Congress Cataloging-in-Publication Data
Gies, Martha, 1944-
 Up all night / Martha Gies.-- 1st ed.
   p. cm.
 ISBN 0-87071-028-1 (alk. paper)
 1. Night people--United States. 2. Night--Social aspects. 3. Night work--
United States. I. Title.
 HM1033 .G55 2004
 305.9--dc22

                          2003022314

OREGON STATE
UNIVERSITY

Oregon State University Press
101 Waldo Hall
Corvallis OR 97331-6407
541-737-3166 • fax 541-737-3170
http://oregonstate.edu/dept/press

Dedication

To Marilyn,
whose friendship made it possible

and to Oscar,
his mother's delight

Up All Night

Contents

Up All Night

Introduction

As I was beginning the research for this book, I asked a Portland cab driver, a salty old Lebanese man, if he ever drove night shift. "No thank you," he said, his dark eyes fixing me with a stare in the rearview mirror. "The bats come out at night."

My own idiosyncratic ideas regarding the night go back to the cover of a 45-rpm record called *Sharkey's Southern Comfort* that my parents brought home from New Orleans. I remember staring deeply into the smoky black-and-white photograph where a cocktail waitress, dressed in bustier, opera hose, and stiletto heels, perches on a barstool and leans wearily into the bar. The world she represented—of all-night clubs, smoking and drinking and jazz—called to me. This is the night of mystery and danger, of solitude and shadow, of music in a minor key.

I also harbor nocturnal images of biblical times, of watchmen shivering and pacing on the town towers, of shepherds camped under the stars with their vulnerable flocks, of sailors standing watch until dawn aboard ship.

Dickens, too, has left his mark: all those lamplighters, policemen, and streetwalkers who populated the London streets, staving off the triple fears of darkness, violence, and an unshared bed. My literary night is populated with Chekhov's watchmen in sheepskin coats, walking the rounds of country estates at night, their warning rattles at the ready; with Hamsun's impoverished youth in rented rooms, going without a fire and fussing with the last bit of candle; with Dinesen's gallant spinsters sipping coffee long after they've sent the maid to bed. Anachronistic nights.

I first worked night shift at age sixteen. It was a summer cannery job at Blue Lake Packers in Salem, Oregon, where I earned one extra nickel an hour for graveyard and another for working the catwalk. Up there under the rafters I made sure the beans kept flowing along the fast-moving conveyor belts, that they didn't jam as they funneled down separate chutes onto the lines below, where women in hairnets picked and sorted. Ten years later, I was the only woman driving nights for Yellow Cab in Oregon's state capital. Still later, during a stint as deputy sheriff, I worked nights at the Marion County jail, booking and supervising inmates.

1

And then—what happened? The enchantment faded, I became a morning person, night fell out of my life. So many college-educated people who have reached middle age tell me, when I ask if they've done night work: *Not any more!*

So who, I asked myself as I began this book, *is still out there?* Coming home from films or cafés at night on the bus, I would see people with lunch boxes and wonder where they were going. There's nothing like a light on over there to make us speculate who's inside and what they're up to.

In choosing the people to interview, I sought a broad cross section— men and women from all four quadrants of the city and from the most populous ethnic groups, which meant conducting one of the interviews in Spanish.

As I researched this book, people generously let me observe them on the job. In assembling the chapters, I have inter-cut my observations of their work with the workers' personal stories and private dreams. I should state that the interviews were taped after hours (that is, during the day), and not during the time I spent with them on the job.

The twentieth century produced a vast documentary literature which, as the century progressed, became more and more self-conscious, as ethnographers came to recognize that their own presence changed the "pure" community they set out to study. In doing this work, I have profited from a careful consideration of the moral and ethical issues for interviewers explored by Dr. Robert Coles in his 1997 book *Doing Documentary Work*.

In the midst of this project, I was asked by a friend, a writer and a passionate leftist, if I were telling the story of the exploitation of the workers. I sensed her disappointment when I answered, "Not unless *they* tell it to me."

Do I believe that night workers are exploited? Some are.

Am I willing to put words into their mouths, to "lead the witness" as my late father, a trial lawyer, would have called it? I am not.

As it will be seen, these workers, while not accustomed to being interviewed, speak eloquently for themselves.

▲

This book is set in Portland, Oregon, where I live, a city flung across both banks of the Willamette River, just south of where it flows into the Columbia. Portland is a young city: it wasn't until 1843 that the first white settlers began felling trees on the west bank of the Willamette. A freshwater port was developed and early fortunes were made in lumber. The only Oregon city of any size, Portland today has a population just over half a million—three times that number when the entire tri-county metropolitan area is counted—and hospitals and colleges are among its largest employers. Intel and Nike, while providing thousands of jobs, are both outside the city limits.

Money Magazine has had Portland in its sights for the last four years, selecting it as the best place to live in 2000, and as one of the top ten places in the nation to vacation in 2002.

Portland's much-vaunted livability is largely due to some hard decisions made back in the seventies, when public and private investment in the downtown core reversed the blight that was the universal legacy of the postwar suburban dream. Parking was reduced, mass transit developed, and a major freeway moved to allow a pedestrian greensward along the river. By the end of the decade, the area had a directly elected regional government which, in addition to coordinating delivery of public services, would control urban sprawl through a system of urban growth boundaries that takes the entire region into account.

Portland's touristic attraction is primarily based on its ease of access to the coast (ninety minutes away) and to the stunning Columbia River Gorge (less than an hour). In a country of polluted cities clogged with motor vehicles, the mere ability to flee is now an advantage in and of itself. Of course the irony is that, given enough people relocating or visiting, that ease of access will disappear. Portlanders are tense about this delicate situation, and a "close the door behind you" attitude is found in even the most recent arrivals.

At first acquaintance, Portland does not appear to be a nocturnal city. To be downtown late on a weeknight, for instance, is to imagine that the city has been evacuated. Even those without homes of their own have long answered the curfew call at the shelters. Here and there a small crowd will appear: the symphony lets out, causing a flurry of motion in the streets between the concert hall and the six-story parking garage; patrons move between two popular bars in the so-called gay district, a one-and-a-half-block stretch at the center of downtown; a noisy gaggle of kids collects outside a popular no-alcohol hip-hop club.

This is not New York, with its twenty-four-hour Times Square, nor New Orleans, where midnight lasts until sun-up, nor Las Vegas, where casino operators have effectively erased the distinction between night and day. In Portland, people are more likely to get to bed early so they can be up and out on a bike or hiking trail in the morning.

But the quiet at Portland's center doesn't mean that nothing's happening: it's just happening elsewhere. Thousands of invisible night workers routinely keep the city machinery running, far from the downtown core. Here, as in every other American city, people are at work in the hospitals, offices, warehouses, and factories; meanwhile, buses, taxis, ambulances, and patrol cars cross and re-cross the city, be it noon, dusk, midnight, or dawn.

There is a universal quality to the rhythms I discovered. These same night jobs exist in other cities where I've lived—Montreal, Seattle, and San Francisco.

In addition to the classic night chores—those related either to emergency services or keeping an eye on things in the dark—many industrial jobs presume shift work, a fact of life in the United States since the Ford Motor Company first introduced line-production methods and fit three "days" into a twenty-four-hour cycle without ever stopping the flow of the product down the line. Today, line work is commonplace and shift work a sign of economic health. When a mill or a plant is doing well, it is said to be "running all three shifts."

While not all cultures accept shift work as a necessary fact of life, here in the United States, where we consider productivity and punctuality essential to the good life, we are willing to subjugate other considerations to the conveyor belt and the clock. We take it for granted that someone, somewhere, is going to be staying up all night on the job.

The people who end up working these shifts do so for a variety of reasons. While I don't think they are so different from their counterparts in other cities, they are, I've come to believe, different from those of us who work in the day. Some describe themselves as metabolically different: they speak of having always been night people, and are simply more comfortable, physically and psychologically, sleeping during the day. Many are new Americans (whether or not the Immigration Service is yet aware of their arrival) in bottom-of-the-ladder jobs. Others are people breaking into well-paying fields by taking a less desirable shift, or people attracted by the wage differential paid at night, or people who are alternating shifts with a spouse in order to save the cost of child care. Almost all of them speak of the relative ease of getting to work when the roadways are clear of commuters.

But it's the relative lack of supervision on night shift that people mention most. They seek the solitude, the retreat of night shift, preferring to work alone, away from the posturing of bosses, the chit-chat of coworkers. As several put it, in the daytime there are inspections, tours, multiple levels of supervision and other "bullshit." At night, there's just the work. For certain people—independent, maverick—this is enough to keep them on night shift for life.

This is the night that most of us know nothing about. We go to bed and sleep, innocent of the baking bread. We give little thought to who stays up to clean our offices or watch over travelers and the sick, in hotels and hospitals. By morning, when we re-emerge, streets and boulevards have been flushed and swept, stars and galaxies have been located and admired, and the morning newspaper has landed conveniently on the porch.

Up All Night

What of the Night?

Watchman, what of the night?
Watchman, what of the night?

Isaiah 21:11

Up All Night
Sativa Dancing Nude

Her stage name is Sativa and she's dancing nights at the Boom Boom Room. Tucked behind the Szechuan Restaurant on Barbur Boulevard, the club is a rectangular black box with an L-shaped bar, a dozen tables, and a stage, all gaudied up with mirrors and chase lighting, where the girls perform. The customers sit in a circle around the meat rack—the low counter which encircles the stage—with their drinks and their money in front of them.

At ten o'clock on a Sunday night in January, there are three dancers working in rotation, each doing three numbers before surrendering the stage to the next girl.

Sativa has a fragile honey-colored beauty, her body slim and tan, her legs shapely. When she unpins her soft brown hair, it falls below her shoulders. Skinny and voluptuous at the same time, she doesn't so much dance as just move lightly and airily around. She chews gum, twirls the way a child might play airplane, lets her clothes drop, then strolls back and forth in the box. Her playfulness translates as innocence, which is exactly what many customers like to believe they're seeing.

Sativa compares the Boom Boom Room to a dark, seedy spider bowl. "I like the seedy places. A lot of the outcasts come in, and for some reason they just radiate toward me. Literally, I attract crazies and freaks. It takes one to know one," she says with a laugh. "I would not say I'm normal by any means.

"You can tell a lot about a girl by how she dances. There's a difference between dancers and strippers. If they present themselves cheap, they're a stripper; if they present themselves with dignity, they're a dancer. Most girls just show what they have. They don't take it as an art form. I don't know if I really consider myself a dancer. I'm very languid. I just fake it, smile, spin.

"I don't feel awake before night time. I've always been a night person, ever since I was a little kid. It's probably just how my internal clock runs. I wake up at nine in the morning every morning, cause I can't sleep past that. And I don't go to sleep till four or five in the morning, even if I do work a day shift. Once a week I'll probably sleep in to like noon, and catch up. But for the most part my body doesn't need that much sleep anymore.

"Night and day, God. The difference is the type of crowd. During the day it's blue-collar workers on lunch break, construction crews on an hour-and-a-half break, landscapers, retired people, or people who own their own business.

"Night shift is a lot of young people, a lot of drug dealers. There's totally two different types of people. There's the nine-to-fivers, the productive people, the normal citizens. Then the freaks come out at night. So many just cracked out or smacked out. People are either just straight-edged or crazy. The straight-edged are usually just manipulated or brainwashed. But night shift is crazy, young, much more carefree.

"People are *crazy* during a full moon. It's just completely insane. Fights happen. They never happen any other time except a full moon. It's like we'll have four days of people trying to get into fights and the cops will have to come. It will be just completely packed or there will be just absolutely no one in there, strange things like that. You never know what's going to happen. For the most part I don't even realize it until I see all these people being strange and I'm like, okay, it must be a full moon. And sure enough, I get outside and there it is.

"I always talk to the cops when they come in. They know right off the bat what I'm all about. They also know that I'm not going to be nice to them just because they are cops. There are some that have come in, gotten their cup of coffee, and sat down not quite at the rack, but like a chair right behind it. You can tell when a dude is like looking at a girl and spacing and thinking about spinning her over. I went up to these two cops one time—they weren't tipping, they were just drooling—and I went like, 'Okay, guys, so how are you spending my tax dollars? You are sitting in this strip club staring at the girls. I have no problem with you guys being in here, I feel safer when you're in here, especially when you're on duty, in your uniform. But if you're going to be in here staring at us, you better pay us, too.' They turned their backs to the stage and didn't watch; they got up twenty minutes later and left. If somebody's not tipping me, then they need to get off my rack."

Sativa is aware of Portland's reputation as having the highest number of strip clubs per capita in the United States. "Houston, there's like maybe seven clubs? Bigger cities, like L.A. there's a few. But anything in California that's full nude is juice bars and no alcohol. And if it's topless and liquor, I think you still have to wear those little nipple covers. That's what a lot of places are, those little nipple coverings and g-strings.

"Alaska only has like maybe five clubs in the entire state, but the money there is extreme. I mean you can work one week and make two thousand, three thousand dollars, but there's a lot of whoring up there. If a chick wants to sleep with somebody for money, that's fine, but that's not for me.

"I only have three women that I consider my friends. They're all dancers. I can't get along with women who aren't dancers because my viewpoints are just so out there most of the time.

"I get along with men much more. It always comes down to the basic thing: to men there are two types of women, women that they *have* slept with and women that they haven't slept with *yet*. And if you're one of the ones they haven't slept with yet, you can get them to do anything you want. They'll *do* basically anything, and that's the way I like to keep it. It's so easy just to play along with a game of 'friends,' but you know it's all bullshit because all they want to do is get in your pants. But as long as you don't go off about some emotional distress or something like that, guys are usually pretty cool.

"Seventy-five percent of the guys ask for my phone number in the first fifteen minutes. I would be more cautious with a guy I met here than on the street. It depends on his conduct in the club. If he has proper etiquette, well then, maybe. But there are a lot of dorks that come in here."

▲

By August, Sativa has left the Boom Boom Room and moved on to a sports bar on SE McLoughlin Boulevard. Vinyl-topped tables, tangerine walls, and chairs molded from stainless steel tubing give the club a fifties look. The rack is in the center of the room, lit with tiny pink lightbulbs.

Sativa comes out in a short black tube dress, along with an ankle bracelet and deadly looking chrome shoes, five-inch mule-style stilettos. She wears a choker and her hair is pinned up with a clip. She moves languidly around the stage to "Inertia Creeps," by Massive Attack. She folds the little black dress below her hips to reveal a jingle bell in her pierced belly button. By the time she gets to her second number, she has stripped to a black bikini, though the huge chrome shoes never come off. Before she gets entirely naked, she introduces a black lace shawl.

Only two customers sit at the rack, at opposite ends, one forty-something and the other ten years older. Both wear white t-shirts that glow under the black light. Four men shoot pool in the back, four more sit at the bar with their back to Sativa, and another is eating at a side table and reading the paper. It's Sunday night and Sativa describes it as "slow as hell."

Sativa has just had her twenty-third birthday.

"I basically have always been an only child, in my mind. I have a stepbrother and a stepsister, older, but up until fourth or fifth grade I was by myself. My mom kept getting married and moving around and breaking up. She's crazy. I don't know my real dad."

Today, Sativa's mother lives somewhere in north Portland, but Sativa hasn't seen her since she was seventeen.

"My mom moved around so much that I never really got into school. I was always out skipping, getting stoned. I'm not stupid by any means. I knew most of the stuff even before I walked into the classroom. Mathematics and science were my only classes that I ever learned anything at. I did not get good marks. I was one of those people who just never fit in anywhere."

She went to three high schools until she finally dropped out altogether and got her GED.

A few years back, Sativa got pregnant and, despite people advising her otherwise, she carried the baby to term and gave it up for adoption.

"It's a lot of trouble, a lot of social isolation," she says today. "I watch these girls that have these babies, and they're like fifteen or sixteen, and they don't have anybody to love and nobody loves them. And they just want somebody to love them, and that's why they keep the baby. For the most part, people are not prepared to have children, mentally, I don't think, until at least twenty-five. That's not an extreme guideline; everybody's different. But in my experience, twenty-five is about the right age.

"I wasn't prepared to give my baby up to some slackers. I got to know the family. I got background and talked to them on the phone, that kind of thing, and told them what my situations were, what had to be done. I made him, I carried him, I gave birth to him, so I do have some say.

"They give me pictures and write like once a year. Part of the stipulation is that he has to know, later on, that he is adopted. And if he wants, he can come and find me. That was part of the agreement with this particular family. If he wants to meet me, he can.

"If he does come to try to find me, the most I would try to be would be an aunt. That kind of a relationship. I could never be his mom. I could be his *mother*, but not his *mom*.

"I gave him up for adoption and then from there I realized I had to start living. So I have been ever since.

"I was actually a floater mechanic for Coliseum Ford. Brake works, fuel line checks, transmission work, miscellaneous diagnostic tests. I was making $7.50 an hour [when minimum wage was $4.75]. I hated it. I didn't like anything about it. I got to drive cool cars. And that was it."

Sativa tried dancing, but didn't like the club and lasted only three days, so she got a job at a clothing store where dancers bought their clothes.

"I didn't take any money home, but I got a whole shitload of boots and stripper clothes, which was kind of cool, but it bothered me because we didn't get paid that much. A lot of dancers would come in to Cathie's and buy clothes so I'd always ask them, 'What's the best place to work at?' I valued their opinion the most because they were the style of girls I like to work with. That plays a big role, *who* I work *with* plays a bigger role than what kind of guys come in.

"Mama Mia's was what I considered my first real job dancing. I worked there for a year and like four months. I worked at Star's for a little while, at Score's in Salem for a brief amount of time, then at the Dolphin for a year, and then at the Boom Boom. I've always worked for just cool people except the Dolphin. But I knew what I was getting into when I started working at that place, cause that place has got *such* a horrible reputation."

Sativa begins a new set to Porno for Pyros. She comes out wearing a navy blue organza sun dress with white elastic straps, her hair loose now below the shoulders. When she sees there's no one at the rack, she shrugs her shoulders and gets playful—she shimmies up the pole, then slides back down into full splits, disappearing below the level of the rack.

A big red-bearded guy in lavender t-shirt and knit cap leaves the pool table and comes over to peer into the box stage to see what became of her. She grins at him and does a head stand. When she gets to her feet again, her little blue sun dress is folded down and she is naked to the waist. The big guy fumbles some money out of the pocket of his baggy pants, hands it to her, then returns to the pool table to make his shot.

"Dancers make anywhere from ten to a thousand dollars a night," Sativa says. "Me personally, depending on the night, it's between a hundred fifty and five hundred. It's a six-hour shift. If there's three girls we do three-song sets, which equals out to be fifteen minutes, roughly. And you're doing them every forty-five minutes to an hour. I don't hustle for table dances. If somebody comes up and asks me for a table dance, I'll do it—twenty bucks per song—but I hate to hustle."

Sativa reads a lot, so some of her earnings go for books. "Right now I'm into Bukowski. I was in a bar drinking one time, and somebody called me a 'Bukowski' cause I did nothing but sit there and read and like analyze everybody in the bar and drink. And it's like, I gotta find out why somebody's calling me that, so I read him and fell in love with it."

The rest of her earnings go toward clothing and recreational fun. "I don't have a car, so cabs. And shoes—I have to have shoes. I buy shoes anywhere, as long as they're cute.

"I quit smoking pot a lot. I don't do any other drugs besides beer. I'm down to like maybe a cigarette or two a day. I used to smoke like a pack a day. Alcohol's worse—alcohol would be a lot harder for me to quit than cigarettes. I can't dance unless I've had at least five beers. I'm so uncoordinated when I'm sober it's disgusting. I've been drinking basically so long now that it's part of my body chemistry now."

So far she's not been able to save any money, but she'd like to go to East-West College of the Healing Arts some day to learn massage and other therapies.

"We all have a plan to get out," she says. "Well, I'd say 90 percent of us have a plan, but it doesn't always happen that way. Sometimes we just get stuck in it. You get older quicker. It really does age you. Our job isn't physically hard, it's just mentally hard because we have to put up with these guys being complete perverts.

"I've seen a lot of twenty-three-year-olds who look like they're fifty. And there's a couple of thirty-year-olds that I work with are just absolutely beautiful. I mean they really keep their body up well and they're very smart. It all depends on how you handle it, but I'd say ten years is a good guideline for most girls.

"There's a lot of people who just run around going, 'I need a husband, I need a husband.' And I've known a lot of girls who have hooked up with people. But if money's the driving factor in any relationship, then it's doomed to not work. Some miracle weird thing may happen, where you're going to fall in love, but if money's the main factor in getting with somebody then you've basically screwed all chances for a real relationship.

"For a very, very small amount of time there was this one guy who came in. He comes into town every once in a while, and he's Middle Eastern, from Amman, Jordan. He likes having a lot of women around, he's very into the harem thing. And one of my friends hooked me up with him. There would be like thirty girls there at all times. He had his favorite three girls that he slept with, but he had the other twenty-some-odd girls that he would still buy just as much stuff and pay for everything and go out and party and play. He was a really fun guy. You had to be *his* though. And so for like three weeks I kind of played that role. And I wasn't his favorite, thank God. I was kind of more his sparring partner. I got probably, I'd say twenty thousand dollars altogether out of him. He bought me so many clothes. He bought me like seven or eight huge suitcases that cost like two hundred bucks each, lots of jewelry, tons of clothes. He bought me like eight ball gowns that I later took back and just exchanged for other clothing. And he paid for an apartment.

"It's very obscure, Amman, but there's a reason why he's so obscure. He does a lot of things that he shouldn't be doing, I later found out. And that's why I separated myself from him. This is like serious international stuff I didn't even want to be associated with. But I actually got to know quite a few of the girls. Some of the girls that he took over to Amman with him, two of them were some of my best friends from high school."

Sativa shimmies up the other pole and slides back down with a broad smile that says, "Whee!"

Suddenly, there's an intense-looking dark young man with a pencil moustache sitting at the rack looking up at her with a sappy, drugged look. He wears a burgundy sweatshirt and white ball cap.

Ten years from now, she says, she'd like to be out of the country. "I never want to be in one place. I don't think I'll ever settle down. Turkey, Amsterdam, Portugal, Spain, Greece, Egypt, Morocco, Australia, New Zealand, Asia. Everywhere, except for Siberia.

"I always figure we're not here to make money, we're here to have fun. That's what life is about. It doesn't matter if you die, as long as you had fun while you were alive."

The big bearded guy lumbers back over from the pool table to the rack, and gets into a conversation with Sativa while she's dancing. As they chat, she deftly removes her white panties—her pubic hair is shaved to a vertical strip. She pulls the blue sun dress, which has been bunched around her hips, back up to her shoulders, takes one of the spaghetti straps in her teeth and shakes her head wildly, like an animal with prey.

Up All Night

Perpetual Adoration at St. Agatha

Two streetlamps illumine the corner of SE 15th Avenue and Nehalem Street in residential Sellwood; otherwise, at three in the morning, the street is dark and silent. On the north side of Nehalem, a single window glows faintly golden in the barn-like wall of St. Agatha Church; on the south side, candlelight can be seen through the window of a small chapel. Once an hour a car glides to the curb and parks.

Inside the chapel a dark-haired paunchy man kneels in front of the altar, praying on his beads. Another man, slighter, with curly blonde hair, sits in one of the chairs, scribbling on a legal pad. They are keeping their scheduled holy hour in front of the Blessed Sacrament, their attention focused on a showy gold-plated vessel called a *monstrance* that sits on top of the altar. The monstrance looks like a big golden sunburst; a small glass window in the center holds a wafer consecrated by a priest.

For Catholics the Eucharist is not only a sacrament to be received in communion, but also a sacrament to be adored: it is the *real* body of Christ. On this crucial distinction, the writer Flannery O'Connor is often quoted: at a dinner party in the fifties somebody referred to the Eucharist as a "symbol," and she replied, "Well, if it's a symbol, to hell with it."

Night and day, someone is always praying in Christ's presence at St. Agatha. They pray every imaginable petition, what with so many worldly sorrows to heal. They pray for children with brain tumors, for spouses with cancer, for lost jobs and lost loves, for the safety of the Sellwood neighborhood, and for the Benedictines who served at the parish for eighty-eight years—and not just the congregation at Mt. Angel, but all the holy men and women under vows everywhere—and for the city of Portland itself, wherever they sense there is pain and need. Without necessarily knowing all the names nor all the details, they pray that the city be consoled, that people sleep restfully in their beds, that night workers finish their shifts without accident, that motorists arrive safely at their destinations, that God extend his protection to people sleeping on the streets and under the bridges, and that the new day dawn in peace.

15

At St. Agatha at least one person must always be present in prayer, since the Blessed Sacrament is on view twenty-four hours around the clock. If the people who have signed up to pray at night cannot keep their commitment, they must notify Emma Bosco, who coordinates the midnight-to-six shift.

To Emma, Perpetual Adoration is so important that she has already planned how she can keep it going all night, should she ever have too few people sign up to pray. "I'll ask for a room upstairs and I'll just stay there," she says. Her idea is that, this way, she wouldn't have to walk back and forth from her house in the middle of the night. "If it comes to that point," she says. "But we've been really lucky. People come."

Emma Bosco, at sixty-two, is still a lovely woman, with long thick glossy black hair and the soft walnut-colored skin of the Tamil people who inhabit south India and northern Sri Lanka. She finds it a great mystery that she ever came halfway around the world, from the riot-torn capital of Sri Lanka, ending up in Sellwood just a block from St. Agatha.

"The Lord blessed me and brought me to this parish," Emma says, speaking in the clipped accent of her country.

As a young girl, Emma lived in Colombo, where her family were the only Tamils in a Sinhalese neighborhood. "Under the British, the Tamil people were well treated. We all lived together and we got on so well." She was sent to a convent school, run by Irish nuns. But in 1958, anti-Tamil riots, encouraged by the Sinhalese Prime Minister, forced more than one hundred thousand Tamil people to flee from their homes in the south, center, and west of the island, and take refuge in the north.

"It was a very troubled country then, in 1958, when it started. They came to rape us," Emma so clearly remembers. A Sinhalese friend, overhearing that their household was about to be attacked "because there were girls there," hurried to warn them. "My mother just told us to run. When we saw this mob coming, we ran for our lives."

Eventually the family was shipped by boat to the Northern Province. "We had lived all our life in Colombo, and then we were just shipped north," Emma recalls. "We went with no clothes, just what we were wearing."

It was a year before the family was able to return to Colombo, where the children could continue their education. Emma, who was already twenty-one in 1959, worked as a stenographer.

Then in the mid-seventies an older brother who had come to Portland offered to sponsor Emma as an immigrant to the United States. She had married in 1965, and Emma and her husband and their two small children, then six and four, came to Oregon in 1976. The family arrived with two hundred dollars and two suitcases.

They lived for one month with Emma's brother until her husband got work washing out drums for a pharmaceutical company, a job which was a big step down for him; in Colombo, he had *managed* his father's pharmaceutical company. They began looking for an apartment in the Sunday *Oregonian* classifieds.

Emma went off to investigate a duplex advertised on SE Miller Street, even though her brother, who lived in prosperous Lake Oswego, advised against renting in the more modest Sellwood neighborhood. From the window of the empty apartment, Emma could see St. Agatha Church and something about it spoke to her. When she learned that St. Agatha was one of two churches in Portland which held Our Lady of Perpetual Help devotions, her heart was set. "They were saying the same prayers that we said at home in Sri Lanka!" Emma says, still incredulous after twenty-six years. "Isn't that something?"

Emma went to work for U.S. Bank as a typist and, within a year, the family found a house to buy on the same street, still within sight of St. Agatha. "Here's my church one block away. I mean that's the biggest miracle in my life. Any time I feel like it, I can just go over there."

Emma believes that *all* the blessings her family has received are because of Perpetual Adoration.

"When we were young, my dad used to take us to adoration on Holy Thursday. He would always pick the worst hours in the night—like one and two in the morning—and he would drag all eight of us kids to this adoration," she says with a soft giggle. "We just went there and mumbled all the prayers that my dad would say." Emma believes that even though the kids didn't understand the Real Presence, just by being there they got something back.

And so today when teenagers ask her what adoration is all about, Emma tells them, "Just go sit there. The very thought that you leave home to spend that hour with the Lord, that's all that matters. 'Oh, I might fall asleep,' they say. I say, 'That's okay. Our Lord understands human needs and He knows people are tired.'"

Yet many of the people who sit in front of the Blessed Sacrament during the night—all of them adults—feel they have been asked by Jesus to keep this watch, as in the Garden of Gethsemane, where he went to pray before his arrest. Three separate times Jesus asked his disciples to stay awake. Three times Peter, James, and John couldn't manage to keep their eyes open, a failure which Christians find particularly heartbreaking, since it would turn out to be Jesus's last night on earth.

Those who rise from their beds in the middle of the night know that sleep is not the only enemy of prayer. Sometimes the will feels powerless to awake the sluggish mind or thaw the frozen heart. Yet they outwait the silence trusting that, from beyond the blackness, God will eventually whisper a word.

Many of the older Catholic devotions—Perpetual Adoration, the established prayers of Our Lady of Perpetual Help, the novenas, the memorized refrains of the rosary—rely primarily on patterns of repetition and silence which were found by earlier generations to powerfully evoke the presence of God. As the Catholic Church in the United States sheds these older devotions, one by one, there are not many places where they are still to be found. That they continue to flourish at St. Agatha, many believe, is because of the nature and depth of Benedictine spirituality. And now that the Benedictines are no longer serving at the parish, some parishioners fear the devotions will be lost.

St. Agatha was originally established by the Mt. Angel order of Benedictines so that the Catholic schoolchildren of the neighborhood wouldn't have to commute two or three miles north to Sacred Heart. "It was a long way for kids to travel," says Joan Gilbertz, a long-time St. Agatha parishioner and self-styled parish historian. She has brought a large stack of clippings, newsletters, and bulletins to her dining-room table and now she hunts through them, finally finding what she was looking for: the cornerstone of St. Agatha School was laid in 1911; the school opened in 1912 with thirty-eight children; the church was dedicated in 1920.

"Fr. John was the first pastor and I think he probably was the one that named it St. Agatha," Joan says. She's not reading now: this part of the story she knows by heart. "Fr. John had a great devotion to St. Agatha. He wound up back at Mt. Angel Abbey near his death, and he wanted to die on St. Agatha's Feast Day, which is February 5th. And, by gosh, he did. There was another priest in the room with him, and Fr. John kept asking what time it was. It was about two or three o'clock in the morning when he passed away—on the Feast of St. Agatha.

"St. Agatha was one of these virgin martyrs," Joan adds. "She's pictured with pliers in her hand. Supposedly they ripped off her breasts because she wouldn't have sexual relations with a king or some dignitary. That's the story, anyway. You know all those martyrs, they have very gruesome stories."

Fr. Cosmas White, who served in the parish for twenty-two years, was the last Benedictine to serve at St. Agatha. In the summer of 1999, the new abbot at Mt. Angel recalled Fr. Cosmas to a parish closer to home.

"I don't think the abbot told us we wouldn't get a Benedictine back," Joan says, recalling the surprise and confusion of those days.

Now the parish is run by the archdiocese, and for many parishioners this is still a hurtful subject. And so this, too, is brought to the Blessed Sacrament, along with every other subject attended by pain.

In the silence of the little adoration chapel, parishioners struggle with their need for reconciliation. *Seventy times seven,* Christ advises us to forgive each other. Four hundred and ninety times we are to extend forgiveness to the sister who quit speaking to us, the nephew who stole money, the wife who lied, the father who deserted the family.

How brief is life on earth! *This* is the lesson of the night: that our lives not be squandered in grudges and misunderstandings. In the candle's flickering light, it is clear that none of it mattered anyway. The adorers pray fervently, pray on their knees, to be able to carry this clarity into the morning, into the daylight encounter, and to feel the same deep understanding that they feel in the dark.

St. Agatha has been a God-filled place not just for the parishioners but for outsiders as well. It was a woman from another parish who actually got Perpetual Adoration started here. Margaret Powell, a trim and energetic woman who stays active through gardening, grandkids, and golf, is an enrolled member of St. Agatha along with two other parishes, including Holy Family, where she raised her sons.

"I always *loved* my faith," Margaret says with enthusiasm. "Even in grade school, I used to get stars on my report card in religion. Maybe not in a lot of other things," she says with a laugh. "In high school, I couldn't get enough religion. I loved to hear anybody talk about God."

It was she who got Fr. Cosmas to listen to a cassette tape describing Perpetual Adoration, and the next day at Mass he said, "I would love to have that in *our* parish, but it's up to the lay people to do it."

At a rosary conference in Washington, D.C., Margaret made contact with an order of priests who propagate the devotion, and made arrangements for one of them to come and speak in Portland.

"And *he* was inspiring," Margaret says. It takes 168 adorers to ensure that someone be present in front of the Blessed Sacrament every hour of the week. The visiting priest passed out applications and signed up one hundred seventy-some people in one weekend—out of about five hundred families in the whole parish. "He did it very scientifically," Margaret recalls. "People indicated the hours that they'd be interested in, the group fell into a pattern, and it just worked out beautifully."

"Well, it was a lot of phoning," she admits. "But it was perfect, because people responded so enthusiastically."

Perpetual adoration began at St. Agatha on Ash Wednesday, 1994, and Margaret Powell can't say enough about the benefits. "The vitality spills over into the parish life. The pastor has told me of so many things that happen because of adoration. The people who go to pray, their own lives change."

Margaret Powell and Emma Bosco are two of the four coordinators, each responsible for a six-hour period. As such, they're the ones who have to find a replacement when the scheduled person can't come.

"Last week I was supposed to find somebody," says Emma, who still blushes to remember. "This guy had taken an absence for six weeks and *I just forgot* Sunday night to call somebody. In the middle of the night—oh my God—I thought of it! And I thought, God, what do I do?"

Since the adorer cannot go home until she or he is replaced, the person on the previous shift can get stuck there if someone doesn't show.

"We have an old lady and also another gentleman who both come from twelve to one," Emma says. "Those two people have been there from the very inception. The next morning, as soon as it got light I ran to the chapel to look at the sign-in sheet: they had stayed *three hours!*

"I called them up and apologized. And they said, 'Don't worry, Emma, maybe Our Lord needed us there for those hours. We were meant to be there.'"

And so Emma's next prayer, offered in the little white chapel on Nehalem Street, in front of the altar, is one of gratitude. How great is God's loving providence. She feels palpably his company in this little room, where the candles burn with a fine yellow flame and the grey April dawn pounds at the windows.

Up All Night

Ships in the Night

The Port of Portland's Terminal 6 sprawls across 488 acres at the confluence of the Willamette and Columbia rivers and is the primary ocean container terminal in Oregon. An entire railroad yard services it, and seven hundred trucks a day drive in and out of it. Seven huge Hitachi cranes loom over the Columbia, discharging and loading up to three ships at a time. At night and from a distance, Terminal 6 glows.

High in the cab of a massive crane sits one of Portland's "night side" crane drivers, Bruce Lyngstad. "A lot of people ask me, 'What do you do? Are you a crane driver? A winch driver, a lift driver?' I say, 'No, I'm a longshoreman.' I like to be identified as a night longshoreman," says Lyngstad, fifty-six, "because that's what I've done all my life. I haven't driven crane all my life. I'm good *now* at what I do, but I've always been a good longshoreman."

For Lyngstad being a good longshoreman means both having the skills to do the job well and a sense of solidarity with fellow International Longshore & Warehouse Union (ILWU) members and with labor around the world.

Bruce Lyngstad's night begins at the ILWU hiring hall, on Front Street across from Terminal 2, where all Portland's dock work originates.

"After twelve noon I can call the hiring hall and listen to the recording and if it tells me there's say like four gangs on a container ship and two gangs downtown on a steel discharge, well, I know I have to be at the hall. It's time for me to go make some money.

"Traditionally, there's more day work than there is night work. And some years are better than others—it's like anything. Usually Port of Portland takes off in October and just goes wide open right through to the first of the year. You make damn near the best part of your year right there. You just work steady. But in the last two years it hasn't happened—Asian flu bug. It'll still have us for another couple of years, I think. That's just my own assessment."

Currently in Local 8, there are twenty-one crane drivers in the night side pool and maybe double that number available for day work. Other work includes winch, truck, and lift driving.

"There's only so many numbers on the night crane board, and it rotates by the number of jobs that are taken up the previous night." If Lyngstad has heard on the recording that a certain number of crane drivers are needed that night and he knows his position on the board, he can tell whether or not all the positions will fill before getting around to his number.

When that happens, Lyngstad explains, "either I go down [to the hall] and hope to get maybe an extra job, that I can hire out for after everybody else is hired, which is a not-too-hot of a job, or I can wait for the next night and hope there's going to be some [crane] work.

"When I go down to the hall, if it isn't the right job or I don't like it or maybe it's the third shift [3:00 a.m. to 8:00 a.m.] or something like that, I'll just get in my car and go home. Maybe [it's] a wheat job. They're dirty and dusty. I might turn one of those down. They're kind of on the low end of the scale."

"When we unload railroad rails from Korea, that's a pretty heavy job," he points out. "It's ninety-foot heavy lifts out of a narrow open hatch and going directly on the rail cars. It's a dangerous job."

Lyngstad, who is beefy and capable, says his favorite work is on the container cranes. "The pay is the best; you get extra hours for driving the crane. And it's just a good job. It's very challenging.

"Not everybody that's on this crane list drives the big Hitachis. This thing's swinging in and out, and you're seventy-five to a hundred feet up above what you're doing down there, and a lot of guys just don't have that. Some guys choose not to; they take *other* jobs.

"You sit up there for four to five hours, you know, you're just going wide open. Some of the guys get carpal." He demonstrates the wrist rotation motion that's required, one hand on the lever to raise and lower the container beam, the other to trolley in and out from the ship. "It isn't a strength thing: it's just constant. It's like two gas pedals all the time. So if you did that for that long of a period, something's going to start aching. A lot of guys, their back starts hurting because of the position you have to sit to look down.

"You just got to have a sense of mechanics and coordination," he says, to be a good crane operator. "And be about half nuts, I think."

▲

For any port, containers are where the action is. Apart from autos, which can be driven on and off the ship, very little is shipped break bulk anymore— that is, loose, or piece by piece.

Garry Whyte, formerly assistant director of marine operations, helped implement the container revolution in Portland, back in 1970. "We took all the money we had and brought one container crane," says Whyte, who retired from the Port in 1979 after twenty-eight years.

The next step was to build a dock substantial enough to withstand the wheel pressure of the massive crane. "No timber dock would ever stand up," Whyte says. "They bought Terminal 2. There was a building and a dock there where they were unloading in the old way, but there was also a space there where we could put this first crane." *They* refers to the City of Portland's Commission of Public Docks, before the city and state entities merged, in 1971, to create the Port of Portland.

"At the time, a lot of grass seed, paper, hides, onions, and wood products were going to Asia," Whyte recalls. "The next step was to prove to Japan it was cheaper to load here in Portland than to truck to Seattle." The strategy worked: within a year, Portland was obliged to buy a second container crane to expedite the loading of ships. With the old, pre-container method, ten to fifteen tons were loaded per hour; using containers, a thousand tons can be loaded in an hour. There was no turning back.

"When the merger happened," Whyte recalls, "Terminal 6 was a big sandpile." In 1974, this sandpile was developed into a major container facility.

The containers, made of steel or aluminum, are typically eight feet wide, eight or eight-and-a-half feet high, and either twenty or forty feet long. Cargo ship capacity is measured by how many of the shorter containers a ship will hold, abbreviated as TEUs (twenty-foot equivalents).

"We started Terminal 6 with two berths, and built it for a capacity of two hundred thousand TEUs per year," Whyte explains. "Now they're putting twice that through a year. We couldn't foresee the explosion," says Whyte, who has followed Port development since his retirement. "These days, if you've got sacks of anything, you put twenty tons together and put it in a container. The only thing that's break bulk anymore is lumber and steel."

▲

Bruce Lyngstad started out in lumber. Born and raised in Astoria, at the mouth of the Columbia River, he worked at a local plywood mill right after high school, then quit that job to become a longshoreman.

"In the sixties the log export boom took off really big and they were towing a lot of logs *out* of Clatsop County, which is Astoria, up to Longview. The longshoremen there in Astoria were a bunch of old Scandinavians, and they went and raised hell [with the Astoria Port Commission] about getting the slips dredged out so that they could load logs, too. So the Port said, 'Okay, we'll bring you a ship.' The stevedore company brought a ship to Astoria and things went really well and then, all of a sudden, we were the best there was on the river at loading logs.

"That's when I started. A lot of us were young. We didn't know anything different. I mean, we all worked hard and got paid pretty well for it and drank all night and went to the hall the next day and got a job and did it all over again."

Lyngstad remembers the Scandinavian old-timers as being radical, and the Finns in particular as being "nuts." Lyngstad's own ancestors come from Norway, from the little town of Lyngstad, which he once visited.

"Anyway, these Scandinavians, they were old guys. They were from the old days of hand-stowing lumber, board-by-board, and the old style of ships. I mean they were *old* guys. They were all starting to retire out, so we had registrations and I got registered.

"I never planned on staying there. I never thought those logs would last that long. I just couldn't believe it. When I started as a kid, we were working on logs that were just huge. And I mean if you fell off one into the water, you couldn't crawl back up. And then eventually those big logs started shrinking, shrinking, shrinking."

When the work dried up in Astoria, Lyngstad began a period of driving from port to port, finding shifts in Portland, Vancouver, Longview, and Coos Bay.

In 1994, Portland's Local 8 opened registration, and Lyngstad transferred up permanently. "I was happy to come to Portland. I knew the city a little bit, I'd been working in Portland enough where I knew pretty much the day guys and some of the night guys. And it was pretty stress-free. There wasn't a lot of inner politics going on and stuff like that. It was a good bunch of guys, I mean nice people, and I really enjoyed that. I didn't want to be in a small port anymore.

"Down there if you didn't hunt and fish and dig clams, there wasn't much to talk about. Up here I work around school teachers, I work around ex-cabdrivers, I work around race-car drivers. I'll be sitting playing cards next to a multi-millionaire that's a longshoreman. Or I'll be playing cards next to a bum, you know, just a street person. You get such a great variety. It really makes it interesting. But no matter what this person is, we've all still got a common bond as members of Local 8 and the ILWU.

"In Astoria, God, we were young and we were driving cranes. We didn't have dock-mounted cranes for a number of years during the log boom, when the ships were smaller. When the log bundles got bigger we used floating water cranes. They were leased from Willamette Western at that time, and some from General Construction. They were certified for sixty, seventy ton. Most of our lifts were anywhere from fifteen to twenty ton. We'd do ten loads an hour.

"I thought, I'll just come up here [to Portland] and production-wise I'll be able to kick ass. I thought I was pretty hot stuff. Well, I found out it took me about two years to get up on top.

"I had to work in what they call the big board [the job pool] for one year. And I had to get certified on these Hitachi cranes. I'd been driving machinery and cranes before, on the ship and off the ship, most of my life, but you had to be certified on this particular crane. A multi-million-dollar piece, you know, they're not just going to stuff anybody up there that says he can drive a crane. So you take a little training program. That was a year later, so I've been doing that for approximately five years now. But now I'm just as productive as the next guy. We compete."

When Lyngstad was younger, back in Astoria, he used to be active in union politics. "Since I came to Portland, I've kind of slacked off. But if I'm directed to take a course of action, I do it."

"To take a course of action" would generally mean a work stoppage of some sort. Since it can cost anywhere up to twenty-five thousand dollars a day to have a ship sit in port, it doesn't happen very often. The last time Terminal 6 was completely closed—and it was only for 48 hours—was in February 1999, when Local 8 went out in support of four berth agents who had been working for nearly three years without a contract.

"When we do these things, it isn't a spur-of-the-moment thing like saying, 'Hey, we're going to shut the port down, that's it, and screw you.' I mean the employers are notified and they'll say, 'Well, it's illegal to do that,' and we say, 'Well, we know that, but this is why we are doing it and that's the way it's going to be. Nobody's going to show up.' But it doesn't happen all that often, believe me. I mean there's laws and stuff, and we can't pull that kind of stuff [very often]."

In the 1999 closure, 150 longshoremen walked off the job in the middle of unloading and loading the *Hanjin Hamburg*, a Korean ship, and the *Yuri Ostrovskiy*, from Vladivostok. Not only were the ships stranded, but cargo got backed up on the river, rails, roads, and warehouses, and in the terminal yard. The berth agents got their contract.

▲

In Astoria, Lyngstad generally worked days, but now that he's come to Portland, he's taken the night shift. He works six to ten, takes an hour for lunch, then works eleven to three in the morning.

"Night time is mellow. There's less politics going on. You just show up on time, do your damn job and go home. There's nothing in between. Daytime, there's always something going on. I don't care if it's a car wreck on the bridge or whatever, there's always something to stress you out a little bit.

"On the night side we get a lot of finish-up on ships, a lot of long nights, but a lot of short ones, too. If you finish before ten o'clock, which is lunch time, you finish the shift and get off work and get paid for it. That's an awful good night. But [going to] five in the morning. The pay is great, I mean you love that, but oh man, I'll tell you, that's just a long time."

"Maybe a little bit more work would be good. I mean sometimes you go a month where you get maybe two nights a week." Other than that, Lyngstad says he has no other wishes, though he adds, with a laugh, "I don't know, maybe a good-looking blonde meeting me when I get out in the parking lot when I get off of work, saying, 'Come on, let's go have lunch.'"

▲

On a clear night in late September, the *Mackinac Bridge* sits at Terminal 6. Although eleven trans-Pacific container companies call at this terminal, tonight only this one ship is in, a "K" Line vessel with a 2,875-TEU capacity. It arrived at 4:00 a.m.; four hours later, at 8:00 a.m., longshoremen began discharging the two to three hundred containers destined for Portland.

Now, two night-shift gangs, one per crane, are in the process of loading four hundred outbound containers onto the ship. The personnel on each gang consists of a supervisor/checker who works the yard with paperwork in hand, directing the flow of the containers, two crane drivers who alternate, five truck drivers and two topside drivers, a walking boss on the ship, four lashers, and a couple of cone setters. The manual labor, what little of it there is at a container port, consists of lashing the containers together with long rods and placing twistlock cones in the corners, both means of securing the containers to the ship and to each other.

Tonight's going to be one of the short nights: at 9:30 p.m., they're almost finished. They'll work past the normal 10:00 p.m. lunch break, in order to go home early.

"When they see a short night, you never seen them work so fast," says Leonard Lamberth, a Port employee who regards the longshoremen with a standoffish respect. "They can do thirty-five container moves an hour. Forty-eight is the record," he says. When they're moving that many containers, "they're smoking."

Lamberth stands on the pier, well back from the potentially lethal cranes, watching the last containers go aboard the *Mackinac Bridge*. "The bays and slots on the ship are numbered," he points out. "The walking boss has a map and is talking to the crane operator from the ship. Every container, somebody's on a walkie-talkie telling him where to put it," Lamberth says, "even though, as the job nears completion, certain placements may be obvious."

The containers themselves, all of which look alike from the outside, can be filled with almost anything. By volume, TVs, tennis shoes, tires, and apparel are among the larger container imports into Portland, while hay bales, onions, cowhides, paper rolls, and frozen french fries are most often going out.

The sequencing of the containers is all done by computer. The heaviest containers get loaded first (but always with an eye to what gets discharged at the next port; you don't want that on bottom). Upstairs in the Port's office, at a "vessel operations" table, everything gets figured out. Tanks carrying flammable material are loaded as far out from the ship's wheelhouse and superstructure as possible. They go aboard in an open-frame steel cage, which effectively turns the cylindrical tank into a rectangle.

High above the ship, Lyngstad operates the Hitachi crane, which is permanently installed on the pier and travels laterally alongside the ship on a track. The long boom is its most conspicuous feature, whether it's at rest and elbowed up at an angle, or extended straight out over the ship.

Lyngstad sits in the cab which hangs below the boom. From there he has a view of the entire ship, the Columbia running east and west on either side of it, and the city of Vancouver, Washington, to the north across the river. When he's working, the only direction Lyngstad looks is down: the cab is clear-bottomed so he has an unobstructed view of the ship and the cargo on the lit pier below.

"Since you're lifting approximately thirty tons every pick, it's something you've got to have a good knack for and a good eye," Lyngstad says. "Especially at night. We have big lights, but still, daylight and dark are two different things. It's just like driving a car."

Another longshoreman has driven a flatbed truck onto the pier, between the ship and the crane. As the driver waits for Lyngstad to lift the full container off his flatbed, other loaded flatbeds queue up behind him.

Lyngstad trollies back along the underbelly of the boom to where he can lower the container beam onto the top of the container on the waiting truck below. The crane has flippers that guide the container beam into the container's top corner pockets. A light on the cab's panel shows Lyngstad when he's securely locked down. After he's plucked the thirty-ton container off the waiting truck bed, he trollies out to nest it neatly onboard ship.

While there's still no room for error, the danger has been minimized with sophisticated equipment, regulated hours, training, equipment upkeep, and a variety of safety regulations. The cranes, for instance, are equipped with sirens, and if the wind gets over a certain speed, the siren goes off to let the operator know it's gusting and possibly a dangerous situation.

Lyngstad has stories about the old days, when loads weren't weighed, or wires were badly spliced, or the ships themselves were dangerous.

"Things were always breaking in the old days. Now everything's changed, and you don't even see those really old ships anymore. I mean they're gone, they're scrap metal.

"Eventually ships started catching up with the modern world. Change came really slow to the waterfront. I guess they figured, it's working so why in the hell change it?"

▲

At 10:25, Lyngstad lowers the last container onto the *Mackinac Bridge*. Done for the night, he taxis the crane down along the pier to where it's out of the way of the loaded ship. He trollies to the rear of the crane and elbows the boom up at an angle. When he leaves the cab, he descends to the dock in an elevator in the crane's left rear leg. A little yellow school bus, the dock shuttle, takes workers back to their parked pick-ups and rigs. Meanwhile, a gear locker crew comes out and locks down the crane with hurricane pins, lest a strong wind move it down the tracks.

On a night like tonight, even though the longshoremen are off by eleven o'clock, it can be tough to find a restaurant still open. "Some of the strip clubs have excellent food," says Lyngstad, who is impressed by the fact that the owner of The Acropolis raises his own beef. "You can go in there and for $3.99 you get a nice piece of beef, cheese bread, and a baked potato served to you and it's delicious."

Sooner or later, Lyngstad's got an hour commute to a home he bought east of Portland. Gone are the days of drinking half the night. "Guys started watching what they were doing when the drinking laws took effect," he says, referring to Oregon's stiff penalty for drunk driving.

While Lyngstad and his friends are eating, the *Mackinac Bridge* is receiving its paperwork from the port—bills of lading indicating which cargo is headed for which ports and what temperature the refrigerated containers require, along with hazardous materials declarations and safety instructions. Tugs assist the departing ship out into the channel. And by the time Lyngstad drives out of town toward Mt. Hood, the ship is heading the opposite direction, already on its one-hundred-mile river voyage west toward the Pacific Ocean.

Up All Night

Rising Star

The two-story brick building, set in Goose Hollow (named for the flocks of wild geese that used to inhabit the neighborhood), was built in 1910 by the Portland Fire Department, but since the late sixties, it has been used as a theater; where the big horse-drawn pumper used to park is now the stage, and the hay loft above serves as dressing rooms.

On a Friday night in October, stage manager Teri McConville sets the nearly bare stage with four green duffel bags, checks what she sees against her clipboard, and calls, "Actors, we're at seven."

"Seven" indicates one hour before the eight o'clock curtain and thirty minutes before McConville will open the house. At her call, five actresses and one actor wander onto the stage in various combinations of costume and street clothes and begin hamstring stretches and neck rolls.

The usher lets someone through the locked door of the empty house: Nora Jesse, a pretty Asian woman, her stylish hair in a neo-flapper bob, scurries up to the stage to join the others. Later she will explain, elated, that she got a callback from a video production company and it made her five minutes late.

Nora takes her place with the others, bouncing, rabbit punching, kick boxing, muttering lines, deep breathing. At some unseen cue, actresses cease their bends and their yoga poses and come together in a circle, where they sing in unison "Proud Mary," the sole man bobbing enthusiastically outside the perimeter.

They begin a speeded-up run-through of the blocking, buzzing as they move, to get the lips alive and awake. The "buzz through" looks like a frenetic ballet—*Actors, we're at fifteen*—each actress deeply seated in her physical memory, turning, running, pacing off the stage.

"We're at ten, actors," McConville announces, with military menace in her voice.

In unison they shout the last stanza of a Gilbert and Sullivan verse from *The Mikado*, another verbal warm-up:

To sit in solemn silence in a dull, dark dock,
In a pestilential prison, with a life-long lock,
Awaiting the sensation of a short, sharp shock,
From a cheap and chippy chopper on a big black block!

They stand shoulder-to-shoulder in a tight circle, humming at each other, with quick, sharp turns of the head.

All the lights come up, house and stage. The cast is sitting in pattycake formation, passing a slap around the circle.

The stage manager calls: "A minute and a half."

Suddenly the flurry stops. The actresses get up off the floor, glance one last time at their props, and leave the stage. They drift toward the back of the house and disappear into the lobby, where they will take the back stairs to their dressing rooms above.

To a silent room, the stage manager announces: "House is open." Around the corner, the usher unlocks the door. When fifty-five people have passed through the door, the show will be sold out.

Tonight's play, Shirley Lauro's *A Piece of My Heart*, was suggested by Keith Walker's 1985 book of the same title. Though the Defense Department kept no record by gender, it is estimated that between fifteen and twenty thousand American women served in Vietnam, as volunteers, as nurses, and in the military. Walker's book was meant to present, through the stories of twenty-six women, a microcosm of those years. Lauro's play, which opened the Manhattan Theatre Club's twentieth season as a premiere, in 1991, further reduces that microcosm to the riveting accounts of six of these women: three enlisted nurses, one USO entertainer, one Red Cross worker and one army intelligence officer.

At eight o'clock, with all the audience seated, the house lights go down, and the actresses take their places in the dark. When the stage lights go up, six women are seen standing at attention, listening to an artillery salute. Each character in turn tells how she happened to end up "in country."

Nora's character, Leeann, is a half-Chinese, half-Italian nurse from New York who joins the Army to get her nursing schooling paid, even though she's a hippy and a peacenik. She thinks she'll go to Hawaii and help heal boys who've been evacuated. Instead, she's sent to Cu Chi, an area forty minutes outside Saigon that was frequently bombed and heavily sprayed with Agent Orange. It's 1968.

"You can make a real contribution for your country in Vietnam," she is told. "And the credit will do wonders for your career—after the War." She is stunned by the carnage. Only when she smokes dope and listens to Led Zeppelin can she relax.

Nora, attractive even in camouflage pants, combat boots, and khaki-colored t-shirt, makes her mark on the audience. When the house lights go up, several people check the program notes, where they read that Nora Jesse has a background in film and video and that this is only her second time on stage.

▲

"I've always been interested in acting," Nora says. "I took drama classes at Mountain View Junior High, out in Aloha." Her first show, in seventh grade, was a comedy by William Gleason called *The Perils of Lulu*.

"I *wanted* to play Ludmilla Linski, Secret Soviet Agent," Nora recalls, "but instead played an android who hijacks an airplane—and has only five lines. Talk about *favoritism*. My junior high drama teacher hated me. I think it was because I was kind of anti-social, I wasn't running with the crowd, but I loved it so much I kept coming back."

She was twenty-four and working on a production line, manufacturing mother boards, when she signed up with an agent. "I'd had *some* experience. I was an extra in a couple of movies that came through town, I answered ads in the paper looking for extras. I'd had exposure to being on a set, at least. That was five years ago.

"My agent encouraged me to get some training, so I signed up for a bunch of acting technique classes. It was definitely helpful when the instructors gave us real-life experience, like what to expect in an audition."

In Portland she gets a few jobs a year, typically industrials, commercials, and PSA's. In 2000, for instance, she did an eight-minute film for Intel Connected Business ("Your voice and data accessible on any network at any time"), playing Tina, a music company executive who is buying a building in Nashville. She had five scenes: walking down the street on her way to work in the morning and taking a call on a PDA; logging on to her computer in her office at Harmonics Worldwide; jogging down the street; and two more scenes back in the office, wrapping up the real estate deal. With hair halfway down her back and a few extra pounds she has since shed, Nora played Tina with charisma, charm, and ease.

Two years ago, when commercials and industrials were few and far between, she turned to live theater. She's a new inductee into the night world.

"Back when I did *Moon Over Buffalo* [June 2001], I wasn't getting work very regularly. It was out in Forest Grove, a very tiny community theater. I had reservations about auditioning, but a friend of mine said, 'What do you have to lose? It's better than sitting around being Nora all the time. If you want to act, then go for it.'

"I learned how draining theater is. I mean even for a light-hearted comedy like that, just the amount of hours you put in for very little payoff—monetary, specifically. I had been doing film, where everything was *paid*."

On a commercial shoot, she can earn a thousand dollars a day.

For *A Piece of My Heart*, she earned seven hundred dollars for nine weeks of performance, split between two runs, and a combined eight weeks of rehearsal.

Meanwhile community theater—and it's unlikely she'll ever do *that* again—pays nothing.

"And so, like theater, why would I want to do a freebie?" Nora asks rhetorically. "Well, it's for the experience.

"I feel most natural doing the comedic role," she explains. "*A Piece of My Heart* was definitely the most challenging acting I've ever done. I'm generally a pretty laid-back person in my own life, and I tend to identify more with humor, so just digging down and finding that vulnerability and that anger was difficult."

▲

"I knew from the get-go that the challenge was going to be finding an Asian American who's really strong," says director Beth Harper.

"I saw everyone in town," she recalls. "I must have looked at a dozen that I never even let read." The problem with so many was they were *from* Asia; whereas the Leeann character is from New York—hip, urban.

"Next I tried the agents. The first one I went to sent me Nora."

The other cast members were drawn from the 2003 graduating class of the Portland Actors Conservatory, which Harper founded in 1985. Since Nora came in as a guest artist, she earned more money than the others.

"But, as I tell the students," Harper says, "'Your goal has got to be *I'm going to be the best actor I can be*; it can't be *I'm going to make a living*.' Unless they leave Portland.

"With Nora, what was really cool: it was a win-win situation. She had a lot of film experience, but you don't get to do *this* that much in Portland," Harper says, meaning the role of a young nurse confronted by the trauma of more mangled bodies than the triage area can handle. "I think the role opened her up," Beth says. "It was like an acting boot camp."

"When we first started rehearsal, I thought they'd ask me first thing," Nora says. "One day we were talking about Vietnamese culture, and Beth was like, 'Oh, by the way, what nationality are you?' And I said, 'I'm Vietnamese.'"

Beth nods: "I think she was one of the last babies airlifted out."

▲

Nora began life as Nhan Le.

"I'm full blooded Vietnamese, the last of three," she says. "My brother is eight years older and my sister six. My dad worked for the U.S. Embassy. Something about transportation—it's funny, my parents don't talk much about their past in Vietnam. We were refugees from the Vietnam War; we left in 1975, November.

"We spent a couple of months on Wake Island, awaiting placement with a host family, and we finally got one in Colby, Kansas." The family came to Oregon when Nora was three, so she has very little memory of Kansas. "I remember a lot of snow," she says.

"When my parents came over here they both had to go to work to rebuild a life for us. His first job was as a picture framer, and I think my mom did a short stint as a seamstress. When we finally came to Oregon, they both went to work for Floating Point Systems, soldering circuit boards. They worked together."

Nora had an isolated childhood. "My brother and sister were in school. My grandmother, my mom's mom, lived with us, but she was blind and she didn't speak any English. I kept myself occupied with my little art projects and my dreams of being a secretary. I wanted to be a secretary! Oh, my gosh, I just remember being home with a babysitter and setting up my little office with stacks of paper.

"I grew up watching reruns of *I Love Lucy*, and I just *love* her. I mean her comic timing: she's a genius. Just genius. I draw so much inspiration from her. She brought me so much joy as a child, you know. Just her willingness to do anything and commit to it. Nothing is ever halfway with her.

"Since I have immigrant parents, they are all about work ethic and getting a very practical, stable job, to pay the bills. I guess I kind of grew up with that mentality, that acting was kind of silly."

In junior high, Nora recalls, her parents didn't want to give her rides to rehearsals nor make her costumes. Her father, however, did see her very first play, *Perils of Lulu*. "'It was good,' was all he said."

Now, of *A Piece of My Heart*, she says, "I'm almost glad that they haven't seen it."

In the second act, set after the war, Leeann is subject to uncontrollable attacks of rage. Like so many who saw service in Vietnam, she has been left to sort out for herself the scarring memories, the public contempt. Unfit for a civilian hospital, she goes from job to job, finally changing her resume so it doesn't reveal she was ever in Vietnam. At the height of her emotional troubles, a black kid in ER calls her a yellow gook bitch and she goes for his throat.

"I think it would really just shock my parents to see me up there attacking this boy and screaming *gook*!"

The play closes with a scene in front of the Vietnam War Memorial, where the women have gone, in November of 1982, for the opening of The Wall. Leeann finds there, on the polished black granite slabs, in the fifty-eight thousand-plus names, and in the arms of a crippled soldier, a coming home.

In Portland, there is always a standing ovation.

▲

After a Friday or Saturday night performance, Nora will often go out with the cast—to Touché to shoot pool and eat pizza, to Good Foot to dance— but if it's Thursday, she'll go home.

Nora's day begins at 6:30 a.m. She commutes for half an hour to Beaverton, where she starts work at eight at St. Mary's Home for Boys, her day job. "I'm the administrative assistant for the residential treatment program. It's a lot of typing and proofreading psychological assessments. We're contractually obligated to produce them; that's how we get reimbursement from the state.

"We have fifty-four beds, and all the boys have some kind of behavioral disorder. Most of them have been placed there by the state, though we do have a couple of private placements. They're anywhere between ten and eighteen years of age. I don't work directly with them, but every once in a while there'll be a boy who will just kind of instantly bond with me. Or be intrigued by me and want to become my friend. They draw me little pictures and come and visit me in my office. Very sweet. But most of them have broken one law or another. They've been adjudicated for something."

Nora works upstairs in the administration building, in a large sunny room. From her cubicle, she has a view of the tree tops across Tualatin Valley Highway. The room is carpeted, tranquil, quiet. The fabric sides of her cube are decorated with cards of appreciation, snapshots of her young niece, a cartoon.

"By next fall I hope to move down to L.A., find an agent, and start working. I *have* to be down there by September or October. I'm going to throw everything I own into my car and head down.

"I honestly think Hollywood's ready for somebody like me. I feel in my *gut*, like deep in my bones, that I'm going to make it.

"I just plan on walking into different agencies. This may seem really naive, but I almost can picture agents fighting over me because I *know* what they're looking for nowadays: they're ready to jump on the next big ethnic thing, you know, the next minority talent. It's okay with me. That's a *good* thing in this industry right now, so I'd better take advantage of it. I'm actually kind of worried that time is running out."

Nora turns thirty in 2004.

But Lucille Ball, she reminds herself, was already forty when the first *I Love Lucy* episode was filmed.

To achieve her goal, Nora has recently given up her apartment and moved in with her brother and her mother (her father, soon to turn seventy, lives with Nora's sister). Nora makes thirty thousand a year at St. Mary's; by living with Duc, she can save three or four hundred dollars a month. She feels she needs to completely pay off her car, a 1998 Honda CRV, and save three to four thousand dollars, before she makes her move.

On a Friday afternoon, she leaves her cube at ten to five, stopping by the mail room to drop a load of work. She pulls out of the St. Mary's parking lot and into the rush-hour traffic on TV Highway, taking the Ross Island Bridge into the Brooklyn neighborhood when she reaches the city. Duc's house is cool, dark, and immaculate inside, the living room and kitchen both looking out over a huge deck shaded by three mature trees. Her petite mother, Josephine, speaks to her in Vietnamese. Duc is still at the office; he works for himself, as a Web designer.

"There's hardly a transition until I actually get to the theater," Nora says, describing her double shift. "I try to eat something if I'm hungry, change my clothes, and go. I have to be there an hour before curtain to do warm-ups."

▲

" **I've heard on the grapevine** that maybe Nora wants to go to L.A.," director Beth Harper says. "I think she has the working knowledge. And she certainly has the ability to risk, to go out on a limb. She's sort of fearless. It's a great combination: a fearless artist and a controlled human being. She's got a ticket to ride if she wants to take it."

"I'm prepared for anything, though," Nora says. "I picture myself getting down there and renting a hole-in-the-wall and sitting with my flashlight in the dark, you know, with no friends and no food.

"I'm ready. I'm ready for that."

Up All Night

Night Bus

At 10:06 on a Tuesday night, Gerhard Blaser leaves 6th and Salmon downtown, northbound, driving the #5 Interstate.

There are fourteen passengers on his bus. A heavy-set man in a suede billed cap carries a *Good News Bible*; a woman with a star tattooed on the back of her neck reads Charles Dickens in Signet Classic paperback, three cellophane-wrapped bouquets of flowers on the seat next to her; and in the seat behind the driver, a girl with multiple gold posts in her ears works the crossword puzzle from a newspaper folded in quarters.

At the Rose Quarter Transit Center, Gary drops one passenger and picks up three more, including a young man wired to a walkman, carrying a Double Gulp. The bus is quiet. People are reading or looking out the windows. Two women are dozing, one with her hand over her eyes.

Through the windows of the bus, the street signs are hard to read in the dark. As he heads northbound on Interstate, Gary calls the stops: "Thompson." "Russell." Though a large man, he has a soft voice. "Kaiser," he calls, then stops there to pick up three more passengers.

"For me it's easier to drive at night because there's less traffic and you're not dealing with all the screaming kids. Not that I can't handle that; I can handle that just fine, but I prefer not to."

Gary can handle most things. He's been a weight lifter since he was eighteen; now, at forty-two, he's pink-cheeked, youthful, balding, and weighs 290 pounds.

There are advantages to having his days free, Gary points out, peering intently through gold-rimmed glasses. "I may get my son to school, then go out and play golf. I can do whatever I want because everybody else is working. I wouldn't take a day job now if they gave it to me."

Every quarter there's a new "sign-up," and Gary gets an opportunity to bid a different route. "All of them are pretty much the same to me," he says. "I have a preference in line, don't get me wrong, but what is more important to me is the time frame. If I can get a run that starts at 3:30 and gets off at 12:30, that's nine hours, but it pays nine and a half.

"Money's never been a problem. I mean, I don't have a lot of it, but I have plenty to get by. I'm better off, I would say, than probably 50 to 60 percent of the population of this country."

Portland's transit system slows down after midnight. "A couple of buses are coming back to the garage as late as 1:30, quarter to two, but they're traveling from a long ways out. If they're coming in from Gresham, they're driving for twenty or thirty minutes back to the garage. But as far as actually being in service, I think the last bus leaves downtown about 1:30.

"They want the buses *off* the road when the bars close. It's one heck of a liability for Tri-Met to have to be on the road while the drunks are getting out. They want us in the yard so we don't get hurt."

At Alberta, he drops two passengers. At Killingsworth, the *Good News Bible* man gets off. "Thank you very much," he says to the driver as he lumbers down the front steps. Three more passengers get on.

What Gary likes least about driving the bus are "the idiots in their cars that don't know how to drive. What I like best is the people," he says. "I think you should treat people the way you want to be treated and better. There's only one reason God put me on this earth, and that was for me to help other people."

At 10:36, Gary arrives at the 7th Street Transit Center in Vancouver, Washington, the north end of his run. He has a twenty-minute break. Tonight, instead of walking, he secures the bus, then goes across the street to Personalities, which is a club for recovering alcoholics. Gary's never had an alcohol problem, but this is the only place open at this time of night. He buys a soft drink and the "bartender" asks him how it's going. On stage, a young woman in jeans and a frayed sweatshirt is at the mike, attempting to sing "Smile." Gary listens politely for a moment while he drinks his soda.

Back across the street, three men are waiting to get on the parked bus: one wears a security officer's uniform, one a suit and tie, and a third reads from a fat textbook titled *Science and Health.* Gary knows two of the men: the security officer just got off shift, and the man in the suit is headed downtown to work the security desk at one of the big office buildings.

"The people I'll pick up now, most of them will be getting off the swing shift." Gary points out that, since there's no bus service late at night, people will drive their own car if graveyard looks as if it might be a short shift. "Day shift and swing shift use Tri-Met a lot more," he says.

Downtown again, Gary has a fifteen-minute layover.

"My natural mother and father are both German," he says. "We started in Worms, on the Rhine River, where Blue Nunn wine started out. There's a lot of wine castles in that area. Martin Luther started the Protestant religion in my home town back in the fourteenth century. The last place we were at was in Nürnberg.

"My stepdad was from Oregon City and he was in the military. He adopted me. We came to Portland in May 1976, when I was nineteen years old." Although Gary still uses German with his mother, he speaks English with no accent.

"We used to spend a lot of time out in Sherwood, where my dad's best friend lived. Every weekend we would go out there and play pinochle. They had cows and a tractor that I could drive. Their car was a '64 Chevy Nova station wagon, and I took it out on their land and drove it through the grass. As long as I didn't go into the creek, they were happy. That's how I learned to drive.

"In 1977 my dad got on at Tri-Met. He had left the [job at a] nursing home to go to Tri-Met, and he told the nursing home about me. So I went to the nursing home in March of '77. I stayed there and worked. The administrator and the owner both loved me. The owner's mom was really, really old and she was about to expire. She wasn't eating anymore. She couldn't have weighed more than seventy pounds. She would get excited when I was in the room, so the nurse asked me, 'Would you mind spending time with her and see if you could get her to eat?' Sure enough, I paid attention to her and she started eating and getting some meat on her bones. At lunch time, as soon as the first tray would come out, I would take it to her and feed her."

Gary left the nursing home job in 1978, then went to Precision Castparts, where he stayed for thirteen years.

"Then I went to another company called Wood Exchange and worked there as a manager, but I wasn't happy. I started thinking about what I really wanted to do. Every job I had, I was always driving as much as I could. Even at Precision, where I was a supervisor, I would drive the forklift. So finally I went and applied at Tri-Met. But they said I couldn't have the job because I needed two years of customer service experience."

He was, however, eligible to drive one of the vans in the Lift Program, which is a shared-ride service for the disabled. "I went there, got my two years, and on October 17 of 1994 I started at Tri-Met.

"I love driving a bus," Gary says. "I wouldn't trade this job for any other job, even if it paid more money. You know how many decisions I make an hour? Estimated? Fifteen hundred! There's a lot going on in a driver's head." He laughs.

Gary's wife works days at Precision Castparts. "Every morning, when she gets up to go to work, I see her for about two minutes. But I talk to her on the phone a couple of times a day. The big night for us is Friday. That's family night."

They are raising a daughter, seventeen, and a son, nine. "I want to stay where I'm at right now, because we don't have to worry about the kids if they get sick. Somebody's always there."

On his last northbound run, he leaves downtown at 11:36 with fifteen passengers, one of them a squalling infant. Two are pale, thin boys with an extra eighteen inches of fabric on the bottom of their jeans. Another man, thin and jaundiced, looks as if he hasn't seen daylight in some years.

At the Rose Quarter, Gary drops one and picks up four. "Russell," he calls softly, a few minutes later. An older woman, well dressed, rings the bell to get off on the dark street under the freeway overpass, and Gary waits until she is safely in her car with the door locked before he pulls away from the curb.

He calls out the names of the major cross streets as he approaches them: "Going … Killingsworth … Portland … Lombard."

In Vancouver there is no layover because the run is over. It's 12:05 in the morning. Gary pulls onto I-5 and heads south toward the Center Garage, where this particular bus will be cleaned and serviced overnight.

As Gary pulls the bus into the yard at SE 17th and Holgate, a man hurries out of the spotter shack, a small structure that looks like a toll booth. He jumps onto the bus, removes the change box, replaces it with an empty box, drops a work order card onto the dashboard, and tells Gary on which of the fifty-one tracks he's supposed to park the bus. Tonight he tries some pleasant conversation, but Gary answers perfunctorily. "I don't like to get into a conversation with him," Gary says, "'cause it holds up the other drivers behind me."

At this time of night, most of the drivers are already in. Gary parks the bus, closes all the windows, then goes to administration—called by some the "bull pen"—and punches out. But rather than go home, Gary gets a cup of coffee and hurries over to begin his workout. Each of the three Tri-Met yards has a gym for employees; the largest, with an indoor track, is here at Center above the maintenance shop.

"I change my clothes, put on my sweats, go into that gym, and I'm lifting weights for an hour. I keep my heart rate between 135 and 145, to make it an aerobic workout. I don't need to look like Charles Atlas because I don't have nobody to impress but God. He's working on me and He's working on everybody else."

▲

Gary's bus, the #5 Interstate, is one of 250 buses that spend the night at Center Street. The entire fleet is spread across the yard, sometimes as many as six deep. There's very little clearance at certain places in the yard, so safety is a big issue.

Tonight the last bus in will be the #14 Hawthorne, which arrives at 2:25 a.m. "Actually," says Geoff Winn, who is servicing supervisor for the yard, "there are only about ninety minutes when all buses are in. Our goal is to get them ready for the a.m. pull-out, which is about 3:45. We put out a clean bus, that has fuel, that's ready for the public.

"It has a great flow to it when it works right," he says, surveying the sea of buses from a high platform above the fuel lanes. "It's basically a bus ballet."

Below, Winn's crew is "shagging" buses around the yard, parking each one where it needs to be for its particular job order, often a regularly scheduled inspection. If there are no additional work order cards on the bus, a shagger drives it through the fuel lanes where, two at a time, the buses get simultaneously fueled with diesel and vacuumed with a two-story vacuum cleaner, called a cyclone. Then a shagger drives the bus through the car wash. Once a week, the entire fleet gets mopped—more often if there is a mess to clean up.

"We've got a geometry to this yard that really confuses new people right off the bat," Winn says. "People can blow circuits trying to learn this. If a spotter doesn't card a bus, or a shagger doesn't remember a card, or if a card gets sucked up by the cyclone. Or if a shagger mis-parks. It's like a great big mobile jigsaw puzzle. There's a lot of ways it can go wrong; the only way it can go right is for everybody to do their job right."

By 2:15 in the morning, Gerhard Blaser has finished his workout, had a shower, and is ready to drive home.

By 2:30 or 3:00, all the buses have been cleaned and fueled, and the yard is finally quiet. The morning sign-out clerk has already walked through the yard with a map, making sure everything is ready for 3:45, when the a.m. pull-out will begin.

Shortly after three o'clock, the first day-shift driver comes onto the yard. He enters the warm lit administration building, where he picks up the pouch containing the day's transfers, and writes his name on the big sign-in sheet. Then he makes his way down the shadowy alleys between the long ranks of parked buses, in search of the 3301. He inspects the outside of the bus, then the inside, where he logs on electronically and sets his route number on the overhead console. He turns on the ignition and tests the lift apparatus and the brakes. He pulls the first batch of transfers out of his pouch, punches them with today's code, and readies them in the metal holder. He fills the overhead rack with schedules, then pulls the bus forward and waits. Behind him, two more drivers are warming up their buses.

At 3:45 exactly, the #33 McLoughlin purrs through the bus yard gates and onto SE 17th Avenue, headed toward the deep southeast, while somewhere, in morning's darkest corner, Gerhard Blaser lies in bed and dreams.

Up All Night

The Chase

When night-dogs run, all sorts of deer are chased.

William Shakespeare
Merry Wives of Windsor

Up All Night

Night Beat

Officer Robert Voepel drives a patrol car from eleven o'clock at night until seven in the morning. He works downtown, where his shift is equally split between chasing drunks and chasing addicts. For the first half of the shift, the bars are open; after 3:00 a.m., the drunks are off the road, and the drug trade gets his attention. Nothing much has changed except the substance and its legal status.

▲

At 11:00 p.m. roll call, eleven officers sit around five tables which form a big square. The average age appears to be thirty-five. There is one woman. All are white.

They are listening as the sergeant assigns cars. Central Precinct covers the so-called "800 area," which is divided into nine districts. Tonight Officer Voepel is given a pie-shaped area from SW 14th to the Willamette River, and from Burnside to Washington, an area he knows well.

The sergeant reads aloud the night's announcements, including information about a recent 7-11 robbery. One of the notices is from Hooper Detox, the only sobering station in three counties. It will be closed Monday and Tuesday nights, the Sergeant reads, in order to paint it.

A question hangs in the room: Monday is the third day of a three-day weekend; Tuesday is both Mardi Gras and Chinese New Year's.

"Alternative location, Sir?" one of the officers finally asks.

The sergeant reads clear to the bottom, then turns the announcement over. It is blank on the other side, and he shrugs.

▲

Voepel, thirty-seven, is tall and fit. Though it's cold tonight, he doesn't wear a jacket because he doesn't like the bulk. Instead, he wears a long-sleeved t-shirt, a bullet-proof vest, and his blue police shirt. "The vest doesn't add that much warmth," he says, "except in summer."

Inside the white patrol car is an MDT (Mobile Data Terminal, that is, a computer screen) and several radios. To distinguish between his hand radio,

44

the police radio, and the radio on which he might listen to a music station, Voepel calls them *pack set, car radio,* and *stereo.* "Nights are good, because the people you're dealing with are not your normal everyday citizens. They're more aggressive, and more—well, let's just say that ordinary working daytime people aren't out taking a walk around the block in Old Town at three o'clock in the morning. It keeps your alert level up.

"We never get a bank robbery call at night. Not as many fraud calls. More hot incident calls like a shooting or an assault in progress. I feel most of it's related to alcohol.

"To be honest, there is no good time to close detox," Voepel says. "It doesn't matter if it's two in the afternoon or two in the morning. I mean, truly, alcohol is a drug. In the seven different categories, it's listed in the central nervous system depressant category. It's such a strange entity: it affects people differently. It's not consistent like the hallucinogens. The initial part of alcohol acts like a stimulant, makes people elevated, and then like a depressant.

"The biggest problem with weekends *is* alcohol," Voepel says. "People drink."

▲

On the job, Voepel is always multitasking: he drives, listens to the car radio, and tries to watch everything on the street. In addition, he listens to the stereo and occasionally checks the MDT.

An emergency call: Voepel floorboards the car, and races from 2nd and Burnside to 4th and Washington, making an illegal left off Burnside, speeding through red lights, and coming south on 4th Avenue, against the traffic.

Arriving on the scene, he finds a drunk, a white man, arguing with a white motorcycle cop and several of the drunk's friends chiming in. As Voepel gets the story, the motorcycle cop was in the midst of giving a citation to a pedestrian when he was interrupted by this drunk bystander, one of a large party of guys at a bachelor party at the Greek Cusina, a popular bar where people break plates and men dance together. The drunk, who had never seen the pedestrian before, didn't want him arrested and started an argument with the cop.

"An officer getting beat up by somebody or fighting somebody—that would be classified as E, emergency response," Voepel points out. But before the argument could escalate to violence, Voepel and two other cars responded, a fellow officer and a sergeant in an unmarked car.

Voepel puts the drunk in the back of his car. The man's friends can't believe that Voepel plans to take him to detox. They are hostile, but as Voepel talks with them, they settle down. "*You* all admit you are drunk. *He* still thinks he's sober." When he lets them talk to their buddy locked in his police car, the men advise him to go along peaceably with the cop.

Voepel takes the drunk man to the Hooper sobering station, where there are two other police cars in the lot. He has to wait outside while Hooper processes two releases, before they let him bring the new man in. The drunk is angry and foul-mouthed and demands to know if Officer Voepel lives in Portland. Voepel doesn't bother to respond.

A radio call comes in for Voepel's area, but he can't take it because he's stuck at detox. After twenty minutes of angry invective, the drunk suddenly apologizes and, again, Voepel doesn't respond.

Inside the sobering station, Hooper staff take the man's blood pressure. A sign in the station: ***Officers, Troopers, Deputies—Make sure your subject is handcuffed until we've had a chance to examine.***

The man can call his family to come and get him—Voepel says they never do—or he can leave on his own when he's sober. Voepel signs for his valuables, which are counted in front of him. The man, who works for a garbage company, was carrying $605 cash.

Later Voepel says, "I'll probably come home some day this week and find garbage all over my lawn. I've arrested somebody from the utility company and found my power cut off. They think nothing of turning in a fake work order. Your phone doesn't work and then you remember, oh, right, I took that phone company guy to detox."

▲

When he responded to the emergency call, Voepel used the air horn. He saves the siren for domestic calls and other fights. "It lets the people know: the police are coming; it's time to break it up. You wouldn't use it for a burglary or a robbery in progress. You want to get there; you don't want to alert people who are doing the crime that the police are there, because they may take hostages. So you have to kind of sneak in there. It's just one of those things that you learn."

▲

It's quiet now, so Voepel heads towards Zupan's, one of the few places he can get a decent sandwich late at night. Coming back downtown, Voepel is flagged down as he passes the Silverado, a club on SW Stark, which runs through Portland's gay district. A flower vendor rushes up to tell Voepel that he has been robbed of thirty dollars' worth of flowers, right off the street. The vendor, a big man in his forties, African American, dressed in a hooded sweatshirt, is angry.

"Some guy tossed them through the window of a moving car, then ran into the Silverado."

Voepel and the flower vendor push their way through the Silverado, which is so packed that it takes about fifteen minutes just to get from the front door to the back. It is the last weekend before Mardi Gras, and most of the men wear strands of colored beads. Many are naked to the waist. The flower vendor can't find anyone who looks like the man who swiped his flowers. All Voepel can do is promise to turn in a report.

"The Silverado security do a really good job containing everyone inside," Voepel says later. "And they're not afraid to call the police or have someone hauled off to detox." While Voepel generally has no complaints against the gay clubs, he does have some questions about the clubs that feature nude dancing.

"We have more strip clubs per capita in Portland—like 250 or 280 dance clubs—than anywhere else in the country. It's a very lucrative business for the gals that do the dancing. They're making a living, they're doing something they're not ashamed of. But the problem is the tag-alongs, the drug and the alcohol problems, the men who go in there, get themselves aroused and then go out and get a prostitute because they need some sort of a sexual fulfillment. Or, even worse yet, go home and abuse their spouse."

Voepel doesn't see much prostitution downtown. "They've gone to E Burnside, all the way up to 82nd, along Sandy Boulevard, up and down 82nd." Nor is it particularly associated with the night. "The businessmen going to work, it's part of their daily routine."

▲

Because it's still quiet, Voepel self-dispatches to an address on SW 1st, on a noise complaint that's already an hour old. "The guy specifically requested contact," the dispatcher says, so Voepel rings the bell even though it's one o'clock in the morning. It's a beautifully restored condo and, after a while, the owner, a white man in a cotton kimono, comes down the stairs. He says that always, outside his window on the weekend nights, he sees car lootings in the parking lots below. "It's those kids from the Quest," he insists, naming a busy under-age club.

Voepel has a nice manner. Though it's freezing and he hasn't been invited inside the door, he doesn't seem hurried. He agrees that the Quest should be shut down.

The man says he's from California and has been here for five years. He complains of Burnside: "Here is the main corridor through a beautiful town, and it's full of bums."

"Talk with your neighborhood association," Voepel advises. In leaving, he says he'll try and check back on that parking lot later tonight.

Later, Voepel says, "Second and Pine is a real problem. The Quest is kids, eighteen to twenty-one, drinking and smoking in the parking lot. You're dealing with youth who don't really have any consequences. That's part of it. Because it's a non-alcoholic club, people go *outside* the club to drink. And the Quest people kind of like close their eyes and go, 'Well, that's not our problem, because they're going out to their vehicles.' In reality, it is, because they're letting these kids back in with alcohol on their breath. You know, they could have a little Breathalyzer machine right there: if you have alcohol on your breath, you can't come in. 'Cause if it's truly non-alcoholic, they should not let people come in with alcohol in their system. That would solve a lot of problems.

"What makes it really bad is there's *kids* that go down there, and kids have that *I'm invincible* attitude. They truly think they can do and say anything and get away with it. It's a good thing to have a great attitude, but when it comes to a confrontation, why get to that point? They haven't learned the art of 'We need to sit down and talk about this.' Violence doesn't get you anywhere except into jail.

"But it does amaze me that people who live in an urban area, they pay a lot of money for a condominium, and then expect [to get rid of] the problem that's been there for *years*. And you're thinking to yourself, they moved into that area because it's an eclectic area—downtown, thriving, urban—and it's almost like they've lost sight of that fact. 'Now that I have *my* condominium, I want all these bad people to go away.'"

▲

Voepel gets a call to SW Park and Stark. He expects a car prowl, but it turns out to be somebody kicking a truck. The principals have gone, and two drunks, both of them white, are left, repeating a story which may or may not have anything to do with what happened. Voepel considers this call related to the Panorama, in that the principals had just come out of the club, which is just now closing.

The Quest is just getting out also, and Voepel drives by the parking lot and checks it. On the bullhorn, Voepel tells the kids: "Turn down your stereos and go home."

"I only arrest people after somebody makes a complaint like that, you know. I'll go and I'll say, 'You need to let people know, let all your friends know, just spread the word, that I'm going to be watching this parking lot.' Zero tolerance type thing. Sometimes it works, sometimes it doesn't.

"There's a couple of other under-age clubs downtown. There's the one, Upfront, at Front and Taylor. Part of it's an underage club and part of it's over twenty-one. I've been to calls there, but usually security has it pretty well lined up. There's not as many youngsters that go to that club. I don't know what it is about the Quest, but it's just been a draw for people who want to act stupid."

▲

Now that the bars have closed, Voepel goes to have a chat with Warren [except for Officer Voepel's, all names have been changed], who is standing on the corner of SW 6th and Burnside, near the U.S. Bancorp skyscraper known as Big Pink. Warren, who looks to be about thirty, is from Oakland, California, and Voepel figures him to be a big-time drug runner. "In the last two or three years, crack cocaine has gone ballistic here," Voepel says. "The people who control it are the black gangsters."

Warren wears a bulky jacket and stands planted on the sidewalk, back from the police. He shows no fear of Voepel, to whom he's talkative and snide. "The police will kill me someday," Warren assures Voepel.

Voepel leaves, shaking his head. "They smoke crack inside the rooms at Cindy's Adult Bookstore," he says. "They've got those video rooms that are twenty-five cents, or something like that, for about a minute-worth of movies. I guess you go in and buy tokens. And then you just drop the tokens in and it makes the movie go on. It's a locked door, so they can go in there and do basically anything they want to do. But I totally disagree with that. I think if somebody wants the right to privacy, go home. Don't come downtown and smoke crack cocaine in a booth." At NW 4th and Burnside, Cindy's occupies the epicenter of the Old Town drug trade.

"North or south of Burnside is pretty much where all the drug sellers are moving back and forth," Voepel says. "It helps just knowing who the people are that we deal with, knowing the names of the guys that sell dope night after night. You just get to know them through contact and stuff. Even some of the guys out there that have fought with me in the past, they don't anymore. They have a different understanding now.

"I'm what they call a DRE, a Drug Recognition Expert. As a DRE, the primary function is to identify people driving under the influence of drugs. It's a national certification.

"You learn about the seven drug categories, the physiological aspects, what they do both mentally and physically to people. A lot of categories have overlapping things, like, for instance, horizontal gaze—that's in the depressants, inhalants, PCP, and sometimes cannabis."

Voepel carries a card with the drug categories listed, along with their primary symptoms. "It tells you all the things you look for when you're evaluating somebody. If you ever see anybody with like pinpoint pupils, the only drug that does that is a narcotic analgesic. If somebody's taking Vicodan or Percodans or Percocets or heroin, methadone, it'll constrict their pupils," Voepel says. "Dilated eyes means amphetamine."

On SW 6th Avenue, Voepel spots someone he knows, a fifty-something black man who is standing under one of the recently planted sidewalk trees. Whenever Voepel talks to anyone on the street, he says, "Take your hands out of your pockets, please. Step back on the curb." To Timothy, he says this almost affectionately.

Timothy follows instructions. "I'm working now," he tells Voepel. "I'm an office clerk at a retirement place in Tigard. I lost my residence."

"Don't fall back into it," Voepel tells Timothy. "You know what gets you back into crack cocaine—people and places. And *this* is the place."

Timothy looks down at the sidewalk before he speaks. "It's difficult when things are not going right. And you feel you just don't have any control."

"I disagree with that," Voepel says sternly. "I think we do have control over our lives."

Timothy stares off across the street and patiently waits for the patrol car to pull away.

▲

I *truly* think that individual officers can make a difference in people's lives," Voepel says. "It's my own personal belief."

The son of a Texas corrections officer, Robert Voepel was brought up around law enforcement. "They had prison farms that actually helped support the state, and they had to *work*, go to the roadsides, swing a sickle to cut the grass down. They're living—they should work for it. I think a lot of people have lost sight of that."

Voepel gets an emergency call to Peterson's, an all-night newsstand on 4th Avenue. There's a man down on the street, and his legs are spasming.

He's on his back with his arms above his head, and his hands are twitching: black fingers drum rat-a-tat-tat on the sidewalk

Paramedics find something in his pocket which identifies him as "Cornell." There are old needle marks on the man's arms, but no fresh ones. "Probably heroin," Voepel says. Cornell never quite comes to, and the paramedics take him away in the ambulance.

Voepel drifts back across Burnside again, where he stops a young couple, a white girl with a black guy. They insist they are clean. But Voepel thinks, from the man's body language, that he's high on crack.

She calls herself "Tiffany," and says she lives in Beaverton. "I have a car and I'm taking him home," she tells Voepel.

"Well, he's on a bar," Voepel tells Tiffany, meaning he's been cited to stay out of the so-called drug-free zone. "If I see him again in thirty minutes, it's an arrest."

Moments later, Voepel gets another emergency call and races to NW Everett and Broadway. According to the dispatcher, medical personnel are in some kind of a fight and need help.

Voepel sees the ambulance parked northbound on Broadway, the back doors flung open, and two astonished paramedics are standing in the street behind the van. They are staring up at the back of their car, where Cornell is sitting up on the cot, raving and wild.

"Oh, no, that fucking idiot," Voepel says when he realizes who it is.

He jumps out of the car with energy, his long legs hitting the pavement at a run.

He stays on the street for ten minutes, persuading Cornell to settle down. "You can go with me, or you can go with them," is Voepel's line, a standard. He doesn't leave until the paramedics get Cornell back on the gurney, this time in restraints.

▲

"The night shift is the best time for me," Voepel says. "You have a focus. My thing is crack cocaine. Middle-class buyers come out in the day. What you see here," Voepel says, at night in Old Town, "is the lower end of the food chain, the hard-core *gotta-have-my-drug* users."

He drives up to the second floor of a parking structure at 5th and Burnside, from where he watches a drug transaction in front of the Chevron service station. "This is a handy stake-out," he says. "Usually, I would be on the fifth floor, with field glasses."

He races back out of the garage and stops the "customer," a young Asian in a red jacket. He's clean. Voepel finds a folded twenty dollar bill, separate from the rest of the money in the guy's wallet, and realizes he was just about to make the exchange, but hadn't done it yet.

Voepel heads the patrol car west on Burnside and, sure enough, overtakes the two white guys he thought were the sellers. While he runs a check on them, he talks them into showing him their crack pipe. It's a glass tube, about four inches long, with a piece of copper Brillo stuck in one end, like a filter. The user can draw smoke without bringing the crack, burning, into the mouth.

There are no outstanding warrants, and Voepel smashes their crack pipe and tells them to get off the street.

"We just did a mission Friday morning," Voepel says, and describes an undercover purchasing operation with marked money buys. "We got twenty-three or twenty-four people, Hispanic sellers, right in this area, SW 3rd Avenue, almost to Burnside." Sometimes the police do the reverse, pretend to sell. "The most buyers we've ever arrested in one day is fifty-one."

He sees a white couple there now, a woman in her forties with a broken-down old man. Voepel has driven by three times in ten minutes, and the couple moves back and forth about a block. Voepel thinks they're buyers who don't know about Friday's bust.

He stops to talk with them, and they contend they're just thinking about going to breakfast. Voepel asks the woman if she ever used drugs, and she says, "Just fly" (meaning marijuana). The man laughs like it's the craziest question in the world. "I'm a drunk!" he insists, as though that were all the alibi he needed.

▲

The last hour of his shift finds Voepel at the waterfront, rousting. His attention is drawn to a suspicious cluster of four people near the public restroom. Nearby, graffiti on the pumping station reads: EAT THE RICH. The two women and one of the men immediately vanish, leaving behind a Hispanic man, who identifies himself as "Jesus."

As Voepel approaches, Jesus casually puts his hands in his pocket. Voepel orders him to pull them back out and put them behind his head. "I was going to show you my knife," Jesus says. Voepel searches, finds an open pocket knife, and flips.

"Your knife was open! Jesus, if you'd pulled that knife out, I'd have shot you."

Voepel also finds a dirty needle on Jesus, an arrestable offense, but he doesn't feel like making an arrest tonight. Besides, Jesus *told* him he had the knife and the needle both.

"Hey, man," Jesus says, "You made me swallow my drugs."

Voepel gives him the lecture: "I don't want to see you down here again. This is a *park*! This is where kids play. I don't want needles down here. I don't want *you* down here. Do you understand?"

Jesus nods.

Voepel gets back into his patrol car. He cruises south along the waterfront and pulls into the parking lot east of Central Precinct. There he switches on a light and starts writing up a report for the stolen flowers.

Up All Night
Sirens

6:46, on a Saturday night in May. Lead paramedic Sarah Blakeslee is in the American Medical Response garage, checking her "car" before going on shift. Even though the ambulance was cleaned and supplies replenished by the departing shift, she double checks, puts things just where *she* wants them.

In her early thirties, Sarah could be a California poster girl, blonde, slim, and healthy. (Indeed, she was raised in the San Diego Mountains and moved with her family to Bend, Oregon, when she was twelve.)

Her shift partner Sara (no "h") Caverly is her physical counterpart, a slender brunette who lives in rural Estacada, thinks of herself as a country girl, and would like to be on the police force someday. Police, fire department, and emergency room staff all refer to these women as "the two Sarahs," and they are remarkable for their contrasting styles of beauty and for the telepathic efficiency with which they work together.

7:16. They go "in service," Blakeslee driving. "Sara always wants to take the first patient," Blakeslee says. "I could care less which one I do, so I'm driving and she starts on the computer. If we get a call, she's responsible for directing us where to go. And then on scene she's in charge of the patient, and I'm in charge of driving. She gets the history and talks with the patient, and I just kind of work around her doing like the IVs and whatever needs to be done. And then we load them. She's in back and I'm driving to the hospital."

At the hospital, the paramedic writes the report—it's still her patient— and the driver cleans up the ambulance. "I'm getting it set for the next one," Blakeslee says. "And then we do the switch." It goes back and forth all night.

Now her partner, sitting in the passenger seat, logs on to the MDT (Mobile Data Terminal), her long elegant fingers flying across the keys.

"After you log on," Blakeslee explains, "dispatch tells you where to go." American Medical Response has a contract to be the sole provider of emergency ambulance transport in Multnomah County. "They have less ambulances at night, probably about twelve," Blakeslee says. "Day shift, it kind of ranges. I'm guessing sixteen, maybe. Always two paramedics per car."

The Sarahs are dispatched to Multnomah and Barbur, one of a dozen "posts" where ambulances wait, forming a doughnut around Multnomah County.

En route, Blakeslee makes a brief stop at Zuka Juice and, five minutes further down the road, at Small's Hamburgers. Tonight, as every night, they're going to be on shift for twelve hours, so it's important to eat.

8:05. They arrive at Post 890, which has "quarters." "Sometimes the posts have quarters, though most of the time it's just street corners," Blakeslee points out. Here the quarters consist of a kitchen, bath, and two rooms, one full of shelving with medical supplies, while the other has a couch, recliner, and TV. A mixed-use fourplex, the building also houses a Farmer's Insurance agent, a masseuse, and a second apartment. In the front room, where the women wait for a call from dispatch, there's a shag carpet and cheap wood paneling; in the kitchen, a microwave and refrigerator. They watch TV and wait.

"When you do go into quarters, you have a pager," Blakeslee says. You have your 800 radio and they can page you on it. You hear this obnoxious beeping—that's your page—and you hit it and the dispatcher will be talking. You can talk to all the hospitals on it, you can talk to the police, you can talk to fire. If you need to get a consult you can talk to a physician."

8:35. A call comes in: they are dispatched to post 630, at NE Sandy and Prescott. But when they go outside and climb into the car, they're told to stay put. They request a switch with another ambulance so they can go to post 840. En route, they pull into the Oregon Health & Science University (OHSU) Hospital, where they need to find a supervisor to sign some paperwork. In the ER, two of the trauma units are occupied, one by a stabbing brought in by AMR coworkers. It's a bad one, multiple stab wounds, and the police are here.

9:12. They leave OHSU and take their position at post 840, near Duniway Park.

9:25. They are bumped out of 840 and dispatched to 825, Sylvan. Blakeslee grumbles about the new dispatch system. "Most paramedics don't like it. These last few months they've changed it so much that I can't even keep track of where I'm going. It used to be that all the medics knew, okay, well, that person's got a call, we need to get going 'cause we need to cover this area. It made sense. But now it's gotten so confusing that we can't keep track of it. We just listen to our dispatcher and they send us wherever. You're constantly driving and you might get a call that's right back where you just started from. It drives me nuts."

In Sylvan, post 835 is a house: quarters are in the basement with a lawyer's office upstairs. They're here five minutes before they're redispatched, and Blakeslee quickly calls her fiancé, Vince, on her cell phone. He works for the fire department and their two schedules (Blakeslee works four days on, four days off) can be such that they go a day or two without seeing each other.

9:41. The Sarahs arrive at post 520, a little brick apartment in north Portland, but before they have a chance to lock up the car and go inside, they are dispatched again to post 135. "There's no good way to get to 135," Blakeslee says, as the ambulance rattles, squeaks, and shudders along, southbound on I-5.

9:47. Now they're dispatched for real, to a cardiac call in north Portland. Blakeslee takes the Coliseum exit, turns the ambulance around, and speeds northbound on I-5. After exiting at Portland Boulevard, she runs on siren at the intersections.

The address they're looking for is a large blue house on a side street, and a fire truck is already parked in front. Usually the fire department is the first responder. "They are in stations," Blakeslee says. "They don't travel around like we do. Their stations are all over the city, and they stay in those areas; any call in their district, they handle. We're always coming from somewhere else.

"They're slowly getting paramedics on all their engines, so hopefully a paramedic stabilizes the patient and transfers care over to us when we arrive. If it's a real critical patient, usually their paramedic comes in with us."

The women each grab a fresh pair of disposable rubber gloves and hurry inside.

The patient, a 276-pound white male, sixty-eight, has chest discomfort and respiratory distress. He's sitting in a wheelchair at the top of a long, turning Victorian staircase, with four firemen arrayed around him. His wife, who called 911, states that he had heart surgery ten days ago at Emanuel Hospital, and this is his second incident since. "I'm okay now," he says. His wife remains unconvinced. "He was coughing and had chest pains," she insists.

The patient is transferred to a stair chair, and two of the firemen help the Sarahs bring him down the stairs, across the lower hall, down more stairs to the walkway, then down more stairs to the sidewalk, where they have the gurney waiting. "Good job, you guys," one of the firemen says to the Sarahs.

10:11. The women get the patient in the ambulance and Blakeslee hops back into the driver's seat. Her partner is in back with the patient, giving him Lasix, which takes water off the lungs.

"Before we ever transport, we find out what hospital we want to go to," Blakeslee explains. "Immediately we ask for the CHORAL status on that hospital. The dispatchers have this computer screen, and it has every single hospital on it and shows whether it's red, yellow, or green."

Now she can see "Emanuel's green" and informs her partner in the back:

"Red is where they completely divert; they have no more room for patients. Yellow is no critical care or no psych beds or no ob-gyn available, that type of thing. If you brought that patient you wouldn't be able to get them up on that floor, so it's better to take them to a hospital that's green."

Because their cardiac patient is stable, and sitting up on the gurney, Blakeslee drives gently and steadily to Emanuel without the siren. Meanwhile, in the back, her partner has got him hooked up to a Lifepak 10, an electrocardiogram monitor, and she's watching his heart. She radios his stats and condition to Emanuel, and then puts a stethoscope on him.

10:21. They wheel the patient into Emanuel Hospital and within three minutes he is in the care of the hospital staff. Her partner does her paperwork in the employee lounge, while Blakeslee cleans the ambulance, readying it for the next patient.

10:48. They leave Emanuel, having made the switch: now Blakeslee works the computer and her partner sits in the driver's seat. They are dispatched to post 825, and her partner heads south on Martin Luther King, towards the Burnside Bridge.

"The majority of the work is going to be your chest pains, where people call ahead of time," Blakeslee says. "But there are those times where they haven't had any chest pain and then suddenly it's a cardiac event. If they were found quickly, and if somebody did CPR on them, depending on their past medical history, a lot of times they have a good chance.

"One of the number one symptoms is denial, especially with the older men. They just, 'Oh, I'm having chest pains but it can't be a heart attack.' And so they'll wait and wait and wait and wait and wait and by the time they finally call us they're almost ready to code. I've had them where we've been trying to get the medication in, but they're always a step ahead of you and they end up coding in front of you."

Code is the word Sarah Blakeslee uses for dying.

"I've had a lot of strokes where they just go quick. They've had an aneurism and right in front of you they start seizing. I think those are worse. You're already kind of attached 'cause you've been talking to this person. Instead of coming in and there's this dead person (they've never talked to you, you don't know them, and you treat them as a dead person): we're going to try to get them back, but it's a body. Versus when you come across someone that's having chest pain, you're talking to them, it's a human being talking to you and all of a sudden they die. Then you personalize it.

"I know on scene some people think we're kind of joking around, but it's almost like it's defensive. We're trying to get things going, but we're also doing that light-hearted talking, where it probably looks strange from the outside, but I think it's our way of staying calm and staying in control and trying to keep that wall up against what's going on. It doesn't always work.

"It helps if you have someone at home you can talk to. Like Vince went to work as a fireman, so that helps. We talk about it at night."

There's a lot to talk about. Being on the street all night, in an ambulance or a fire truck, she and Vince both see things that other people don't see.

"Most people don't see all the assault and the drug and the alcohol abuse. They don't see the transients, who tend to hide or stay in a warm spot. They're under the bridges, like the Burnside. There's a spot under the Fremont Bridge. It's amazing—they have their own little cities and homes. People are busy driving around, driving to their job, driving home, they don't see like the homeless teens."

11:18. They arrive at 825, having made a brief stop to pick up salads at Zupan's, one of two downtown groceries that stays open all night. Since there are no quarters at 825, they park near the Sylvan Plaid Pantry and wait in the car.

11:39. They are dispatched to post 630, 91st and Sandy, but as soon as her partner sets out, they are sent back again by dispatch. Blakeslee mutters that this new dispatching system is "a mess."

"When we get a call, we're supposed to be there within eight minutes," Blakeslee says. "We have this geography training so we learn how the city's set up. But with having to cover so many different areas, it's almost …" She trails off in frustration.

As a hedge against getting lost, all ambulances carry a Thomas Guide. "Just get the map out," Blakeslee says. "Or prevent it by getting the map out right away. But like southwest hills, those map books aren't correct. That's been a huge problem that we've been trying to work on with the Thomas Brothers, 'cause they'll have a street that on the map book it shows it goes through, but up there there's no such street."

11:44. Back at post 825, Sara Caverly parks the car near the German-American School and pulls out her novel, Orwell's *1984*. Sarah Blakeslee works the crossword puzzle from a newspaper.

12:05. They are dispatched back to post 840, and her partner starts up the car.

12:12. When they arrive back at post 840, the basement quarters beneath the lawyer's office, neither Sarah gets out. Caverly sits at the wheel with the motor running and a single light focused on her novel. It's turning out to be a slow night.

"On nights it's mostly the auto accidents," Blakeslee says, "which usually involve drunk driving. We see a lot of that. Or drunks on the street, transients that are past the point to where they can really go to detox. We can't take them if they've been bleeding, if they've fallen down and hit their head.

"You see the heroin overdoses. You see more of the assaults. You see suicide attempts more, I think, at night. You see the cardiacs, usually in the morning. For some reason, unless it's really bad, people try and wait: *okay, now it's six o'clock, now it's okay to call.*"

▲

After earning a degree in psychology and health from Linfield College in 1989, Sarah Blakeslee was uncertain about a career. She worked for a year in medical weight-loss counseling and realized it wasn't right for her. "I wanted to get into something with para-medicine," she explains. She enrolled at Portland Community College and earned her EMT Basic. She was working as a front-desk reservations clerk at the Marriott Hotel, where management liked as many of the staff as possible to know first aid. "Anytime there was an emergency they'd page and have you come up."

In 1991, she began driving for Care Ambulance, continued her coursework in a private school, and passed her paramedic exam. Two years later, she went over to AMR, which subsequently won its contract with the county, in 1995. She drove long-distance transport waiting for a lead medic shift to open up, and when it did, it happened to be the 7:00 p.m. to 7:00 a.m. shift. "I've been on night shift for about a year and a half now," she says.

12:21. Lights and siren! They are dispatched to a north Portland heroin overdose, and they race northbound on I-5.

"Probably the most common medication we give is Narcan, for reversing the heroin. I've had several times where, no matter what you do, they just end up dying. Some of the heroin is so strong or whatever they mix it with—we're seeing them where they've cut it I think with like arsenic—they'll end up having pulmonary edema, so there's fluid on their lungs.

"Nowadays, on any overdose they send police right away because of the chance that it could get violent, like if they're real suicidal and don't want help, and somebody else has called.

"You see a wide range. You see a lot of the ones who probably used to be career people but they're transient because it's at that point. They lose their job, they lose their family, they lose everything. And so they end up being on the streets. With heroin, I'd say the most popular age is thirties to forties, but we see the young ones, the old ones."

12:31. They arrive to find a fire truck parked outside, and make their way along the side of a house, looking for the entrance to an apartment.

The basement apartment has heat ducts and other mechanicals running around the low ceiling. The door through which the women enter is the only way in or out, and one of the firemen (all of whom seem so tall down here) points out that the dwelling is illegal. Several people are here, including a heavy-set hysterical woman who made the 911 call, a couple of friends, and a pit bull named Glory. Along with the four firemen, there are a couple of cops here, one of them female.

"Ted" is lying on the bed in the bedroom, and the four firemen are standing around, trying to keep him awake. They've already given him Narcan, but he's lapsing into sleep and annoyed to be roused. No, he decidedly did not overdose. "Bullshit!" he says. Ted's a bantam-weight white guy, fifty-three. He's outraged at the crowd gathered here and refuses to go *anywhere* in an ambulance. The woman keeps screaming, "You overdosed again!" Ted denies even being a user.

The male cop moves all the people into the living room so that his partner can have a moment alone with Ted. Mincing no words, she gives Ted the option of going to jail with her or to the hospital with the ambulance, no criminal charges pressed. He decides to go with the ambulance after all.

12:44. They depart the scene. Blakeslee is in back, keeping an eye on Ted. He says he's cold, and she gets him an extra blanket, then starts him on oxygen. "Emanuel's green," her partner tells her from the driver's seat.

12:59. They arrive at Emanuel Hospital and transfer Ted to ER staff. Blakeslee fills out the paperwork, while her partner cleans out the car.

Just as they're both ready to clear the hospital, a woman comes lumbering in through the emergency room doors, heavy with labor. With her is a bewildered husband, carrying a toddler. Before the hospital staff even spot her, the two Sarahs pull her into an empty ER room, get her down on a gurney and yank the curtains shut in front of her. They both moved at once, without consultation.

"After a while it gets to that point where you don't even have to talk, you know what the person's going to do, how they approach patients and how you can work along beside them. It took maybe a month or two months, and then we kind of settled in. You become so close because you're working like twelve hours straight. It's almost like a marriage. I can look in back and see just by her face what's going on, if she needs help or if this person's giving her a bad time. But I think you develop that. I think everybody eventually does if they've been working together for quite a while."

Within one minute they are relieved by ER staff. Though the ambulance paramedics don't like to deliver babies, there are times when it can't be avoided. *"Please contact Donna whenever a crew delivers a baby,"* reads a sign posted at the AMR office. Donna Lehmann edits *The Parascope*, the AMR employee newsletter, and wants to make sure that no heroics go unsung.

1:32. The Sarahs clear Emanuel and are dispatched to the brick apartment complex at post 520, Blakeslee driving. On her way, she drives a four-block square (north on Interstate, east on Killingsworth, south on Vancouver, west on Alberta), looking to check the street action. Seeing none, she decides it's *really* a quiet night.

After driving for five years, Sara Caverly is still outraged to think that the Oregon Health Plan pays for heroin-related care—ambulance rides for an overdose, methadone dosages in a treatment program—but balks at paying for cancer treatment for people who are really sick, patients who are considered to be at the end of their life.

"Yeah, when you're in this job you get very pissed with the Oregon Health Plan," Blakeslee concedes. "Though, actually I've heard that things are changing now. I think there is a little less sympathy for the addicts. And especially heroin—it's such an addictive drug. I don't know their home life, I don't know how they grew up. But at the same time they *chose*. I think everybody's had some difficult issues in their lives, where they chose *not* to go to the alcohol or go to the drugs.

"Sympathy depends on how the person's treating you, too. Because most of them are cussing and they'll hit us, they'll spit at us. When they're like that you get angry 'cause here you just saved their lives and they don't care. At the same time, it could be the drug talking."

1:47. They arrive back at post 520 and go indoors and sit.

2:04. They are dispatched to 135, Gresham, off Powell and Eastman Parkway. En route they stop at Taco Bell.

3:02. Dispatched to 105, SE Stark and 181st.

3:24. Dispatched to post 220 in Gresham, Krueger's Truck Stop.

3:54. Dispatched to post 105, a nice two-bedroom apartment.

4:12. Dispatched back to 220. The Sarahs are annoyed. "Why don't they let us just stay put? Why bother to maintain quarters for the drivers if there's no intention of using them?"

4:21. This time Blakeslee parks at Legacy Mt. Hood Medical Center, which is the alternative to Krueger's Truck Stop at post 220. This has been an extremely slow Saturday night. And yet she doesn't actually want it to be busy because when it's busy, people are getting hurt.

5:30. Dozing: crossword puzzle finished, novel finished; coffee cold, fruit ripening, and sandwiches going stale in plastic bags. For some reason, dispatch has left them alone. Day breaks.

6:07. They can head back toward the AMR garage, at SE 2nd and Ankeny. Sarah Blakeslee would like to go running this morning at Glendoveer, if they don't get a late morning call before their shift ends at seven o'clock. She starts the engine and begins to head west.

Up All Night

The Legendary Judie Brown

Judie Brown is a huge woman in her early fifties. She wears a Mickey Mouse wristwatch, has her hair whacked off in a bob, and drives a Cadillac Eldorado when she's not driving cab. She's a legend among taxi drivers, both for driving nights in north Portland and for the violence she's survived. Through it all, she has remained fearless. As she puts it, "It happened that I'd been mugged, shot, stabbed. So what was going to happen again? The law of limitations had already took effect." And she laughs the laugh of a big, salty woman.

"I was two weeks on the job and I was mugged," Judie explains. "The guy mugs me, jumps out, and runs away. There was a cop across the street hassling a hooker, but I didn't ask for any help; I didn't scream, 'Help me!'

"It was like one, two o'clock. The guy said, 'Let me out here,' and then, all of a sudden, he pushed me and reached in my pocket. But he only got twenty bucks. He thought he'd get more money, but he didn't. He just got my change. But I got really mad. If they hadn't had those dividers I would have ran the guy down.

"The supervisor pulled me into the Shamrock and kept me there all night, talking to me. I said, 'Would you please let me go make some money? Let me go *see* if I can.'

"To make money at it, I think you need to have a knowledge of the city. You need to know where people want to go. You have a different diversity of people getting in and saying, 'I want to do this. Where can I do it at?'

"They want to dance, I ask them if they want jazz, western, retro. They used to have a place called Rockin' Rodeo which would be a good place to go dancing western, but now I take 'em out to the Ponderosa at Jubitz. Jazz D'Opus is a good place to go for jazz, but the Candlelight Room has the best music. Key Largo used to be a fun place to dance. I don't know why is it the owner decided to change the name to Om. Another fun place to go if you like Cuban culture and music is La Bamba.

"They want to eat, it depends what time of day and what side of the city we're on. If they get in [the cab] at three o'clock in the morning, there's very few selections besides Denny's, Shari's, Carrow's, the Hotcake House. The best quote I heard about the Hotcake House was: *At night time the most famous people have thrown up in their toilet.*

"So you need to know the basic layout of the city and have good communication skills. That would give you good tips. We have cab drivers that don't know their way around and don't speak English. And they put them behind the wheel *of a cab*!

"Up until three years ago, north, northeast used to be always busy. A lot of businesses, a lot of people. I've had calls where they wanted to go from one bar down to a bar one block away. From the Paragon Club to the Jockey Club, and he called a cab. I did it, but I bitched the whole way. It was $2.60. It's only ten cents a block. The guy was so drunk, really messed up. He thought he was going to be generous and he handed me three dollars. And he got out and the bottom bill was a twenty dollar bill. That's his problem.

"We used to be able to carry alcohol and sell it, up to about five years ago. This side of town, there was always somebody that would be wanting a bottle. There was a few of them that would do this on a regular basis, and so you'd have it on hand. All you had to do was go to the trunk of your car. Then the OLCC [Oregon Liquor Control Commission] came down with an edict: *If you don't have a liquor license you can't sell it.*

"We used to do shopping, too, like somebody wanted us to go to the grocery store. Then the OLCC said you could not even go to the store and *buy* the alcohol. If *they* want to go, we can pick them up, we can take *them* to the store and *they* can buy it.

"It used to be, if somebody'd run out of gas, they'd call and you'd just do it yourself. But now, you can't do that. You can't have a gas can in your car and do a gas run.

"I can get a fifteen dollar cigarette run. This one woman wanted a cigarette so bad that she was willing to pay delivery price and it turned out to be fifteen dollars. For a pack of cigarettes! And she could have walked the two and a half blocks. She said, 'I just need a cigarette. I haven't smoked in three years.' I said, 'Why now?'

"A night-time thing is picking up a woman or a man who's out looking for their respective spouse. They know who they're cheating with, they know what they're looking for, sometimes they even know what house. And they just keep it up. If it's a woman looking for a man and they start bitch, bitch, bitch, bitch, bitch, bitch, bitch. And I just come up and, 'Why do you put up with it?'

"Men, they just sit there and they whine.

"I took a lady to a new private house about 12th and Killingsworth. She was rather drunk, and she was going to get *her man*. She went to the door and the lock was changed. She beat on it and pounded on it. She was a native African. I thought I would get the money from him, but she got into the house and they beat the shit out of her. In Africa they feel they have the right to do that. And he came out to pay me and all he had wrapped around him was a towel. He was buck naked. He paid me and I called the cops.

"I've called the cops a couple times. Or I would have dispatch do it. You run into a lot of different people. You name it, I've probably picked it up.

"The fares are different at night. The same person who has a three-piece suit and a corn cob up his butt in the daytime puts on his Bally loafers and goes out and lets his hair down and gets drunker than a skunk and chases women and cheats on his wife. But during the daytime he's supposed to be an upstanding citizen.

"Lot of the jobs in the daytime are charged to an account. You have business deliveries, you have school trips, you have Tri-Mets, you have medical—they're all paper.

"Night time most of it's cash. It's usually people out for a good time, or going shopping, or getting from point A to point B. There are people going to work because they work that late shift. Some people work in the buildings, like engineers or janitorial. They work at the post office. They work at hospitals, bars, restaurants.

"I drive seven days, start at seven [p.m.] and usually stay out until six or seven o'clock.

"The reason I work that much is cause I need a lot of money. [One of my sons] is twenty-four, the other one's twenty-five. My daughter's twenty-three. Their partners are twenty-two and twenty-one. Then I have a five-year-old grandson and a three-year-old grandson. When I had my grandchildren, I'd get them to school, sleep while they were at school, and I'd get them from school. Basically I only need four hours of sleep. Sometimes I catch two hours of sleep between 2:30 and 5:00.

"We're set up for the big airport runs. They start between 4:30 and 5:00. A lot of them are time calls.

"I try to stay awake with Coke because it's carbonated sugar. But twelve hours a day *sitting there*. You have twelve, thirteen hours in the cab, four hours of sleep, that leaves you seven hours a day. You're really not wanting to go out and exercise. And it's the quick meals, the stuff that doesn't get digested. Everybody gains weight—except for a few high-metabolism people who stay skinny as a rail. I think I gained over a hundred pounds."

▲

"I was shot. It was the 6th of July, four years ago. Basically what happened was I was forced to go, at 2:30 in the morning, to Pizza Hut on Lombard and Williams. I told the dispatcher, 'There's nobody there. It closed down at ten o'clock.'

"But I was forced to go there by the dispatcher. It was supposed to be a woman corner call—somebody had called in and said she was going to be standing outside on the corner.

"I was headed east on Lombard, I'd just passed Williams. I could have turned onto Williams but I didn't. I decided to go on to Taco Bell. It was a hot night and I—something told me to put up my window. So I put up my window and the next thing I know, as I drove by Pizza Hut my window imploded. It just went all shattered.

"I pulled over as quick as possible. I pushed the emergency button. There's a little specific button you hit on there, and it will give off a loud alarm at the main dispatch office. It runs off the satellite dish; that's the reason why you don't hear a radio on. They can tell within about three feet where the cab's at if the locator thing is working.

"I pinpointed where the shot came from. He was like by Mary Jane's [Cafe], on that [north] side. And it wasn't until I was sitting there that I knew I'd been hit because my coat was wet.

"This other night lady driver, Cindy, she was downtown and she'd heard I'd been hit—she beat the cops there.

"It took the cops twenty minutes to come! And then they wouldn't approach the car. I was sitting in my cab. The policeman that got there, he says, 'Where are they?'

"And I says, 'About three blocks up. You know, you're a little late.'

"And then they said something—this was really strange—about wanting to search. And I said, 'Well, let me see. You want to search *me*? I'm the one that got hit.' Sometimes I wonder.

"They searched my cab, but they couldn't find the plug. They didn't have a clue. They literally *tore it apart* looking for a plug, and they couldn't find it.

"I would say the caliber was about a 45, for the simple reason that after that night I had a round burn mark right by the voice box that stayed for three weeks. I think it hit my throat and bounced back out. It was really strange.

"I was taken to the hospital, Woodland Park, out there in Gateway. They had Cindy take me. And she was in such a state. She wasn't going to shut up until she took me to the hospital.

"Because of the other things that happened that night, I think it was a gang initiation. Because they had shot at a police car and what I would call a civilian car. Later on, about 4:30 in the morning, they caught the shooter. They got plugs from them. So they prosecuted for those two. But they couldn't find the plug for me, so they couldn't do anything.

"But they impounded my car for two days—I was down for two days."

▲

"I was born in 1945, in Portland, but I lived in Eugene. I came [back] to Portland in '64 to school, Western Business School. It was right above where John Helmer's is," she says, referring to a family-run haberdashery that's been in downtown Portland since the twenties. "I went there for an IBM course which turned out to be IBM *keypunch.* There was a lot of things I didn't know. I was a regular country bumpkin that didn't know squat, and they lied to me.

"I did a small stint in Alaska. My first husband took me to Arizona for about six months. Phoenix. I lived in Scottsdale, Tempe, Mesa, and Phoenix all in that short period of time. And I spent a *long time* in Athens, Texas. It's the capital of Henderson County, seventy-five miles southeast of Dallas.

"I've worked janitorial graveyard. I've worked warehouses. Working nights is just something I like to do. But the warehouse and I had a parting of the ways.

"I started looking in the newspaper, the first thing I saw was cab driver. So I went and applied. What Broadway does is they run cabby college, and all the rest of the companies refer [drivers] to Broadway to learn. So instead of being selective, Broadway takes all comers. About everyone that drives Green Cab, White Van, and Ready Ride has been at Broadway at one time or another.

"Anyway, I went up to the interview with George [Van Hoomissen, the owner]. He said, 'You want days?' I said, 'No. I don't like days. I'm not a day person.' And he looked at me strange, and I said, 'I want a station wagon and I want to work nights.'

"They usually don't put women on nights. You kind of have to request it. There was another one that came later on, and she worked all night, too. But generally women will work four in the morning and then they'll quit in the afternoon; or they'll start at seven or noon or something and quit before midnight. Before things really get weird.

"I started in March, that'd be '93. But I almost didn't start because I had a young family. Being a single parent, I wanted a guarantee. That's when

George called me personally and talked to me. I was kind of impressed with that. But I said, 'I don't know if I can do this because you can't guarantee anything. I have a family.' And so he said, 'Well, there's two things you do best, talk and drive. What have you got to lose? You have the first X amount of days free.'

"So I started. And you know, I went right to it, like a fish jumping in the water. The first night I made $117, which is unheard-of for somebody new.

"I love driving, I always have. I had a little Jetta that I loved, going 140 down the road. But my mother was in a wheelchair. She had a really hard time getting in and out of that Jetta. I got the Cadillac Eldorado because of her. You open *this* door, you can almost drive a pickup in it. I picked it up at $1,300, stuck another thousand into it. It's a great road car. I just got back from Coeur d'Alene, one tank full of gas from here to there.

"Anyway, they had told me to start downtown, but I just wandered over to where I knew my territory. I'm talking about St. John's, Kenton, Albina, what they call the Hood.

"There was two Radios and three Broadways that worked that area. The five guys, they all knew each other. They sat back for two weeks and watched me. They figured that I would get scared, but when I didn't, when I was making money, they decided to give me some good tips. Where the Adidas store is right now, there on Alberta and MLK, it used to be a vacant lot, and we all used to sit there and talk to each other.

"One thing I hear it all the time—you just sort of chuckle—is, 'Doesn't this scare you?' I say, 'Now let me see. You got in my cab. I could be a psycho maniac. I could be out to kill you. Does it scare *you*?' I get these strange quiet, 'Well, uh …' It works both ways.

"St. Johns, I usually got nothing but trouble. Most of the people that ran on me or stiffed me came out of St. Johns. I wouldn't say it's exactly tough, I'd just say I had the worst luck there. We had a driver named Frenchie who would only work St. Johns to Interstate. He wouldn't come across Interstate; he didn't have good luck here. And me, I didn't want to run to St. Johns.

"Getting stabbed was kind of strange. I got sent out to St. Johns, the Shamrock Market, Oswego and Fessenden. This had to be 1996. It was another two or three o'clock in the morning. And I said, 'I really don't want to go.' But it was slow, nothing was going on and business hadn't been so good.

"This guy, he went all the way around the car to get in behind me. Okay, so I said, 'Sir, you cannot sit behind me. You're going to have to scoot over.' So he scooted over. And then he told me he wanted to go to Pier Park Apartments, which is on Columbia. So I went up onto Fessenden and turned around, because you get to it by Oswego; it was less than a mile away. They sent me all that way for a three-dollar order.

"And out of the corner of my eye—I have great peripheral vision—I see this blade coming at me. About that time I jammed both feet on my brake and I grabbed the knife. I grabbed the blade. He comes flying forward, and I'm fighting for the blade and trying to hit the emergency button. He did not ask me for squat. He just told me, "Drive, bitch."

"I threw it in park, grabbed my cell phone, and popped open my door. I was stepping out, 'cause if he was going to kill me, they were going to find me.

"And he got out and ran like hell. It had started raining.

"He was a very nice-looking black kid, nicely dressed, well spoken. I would say he was in his early twenties. But the big tipoff was his going out of his way to get behind me. If somebody gets in behind me, even if they appear to be nice, the hairs go up on the back of my neck. Or usually with me it's a feeling in the pit of my stomach.

"Even from the time I was little, I would *see* things and they would happen. It was like a premonition. I would see it, it would happen. Maybe the next day, the next hour, the next week, the next year. Driving places that I might go. Somebody calling. It used to freak me out.

"Anyway, after I was stabbed, I drove myself to the hospital. The best hospital is Adventist Hospital, but it takes too long [to get there]. I went to Woodland Park. I walked in and they said, 'What can we do for you?' I said, 'Oh, I've been stabbed.' They looked at me and they said, 'Let's see, you were shot a couple years ago …'

"He had sliced my hand and I needed stitches. Then I went back to work.

"Three years ago the business went really bad in northeast. It was affordable nice housing that could be upgraded and the price of a home over here started going sky high. Yuppies started moving in and a lot of the other people started moving out.

"One night I was the only driver there, covering five northeast zones, and getting no orders. I did not get one job in two hours. I said, 'I could have sat two hours and at least got nine dollars out at the airport.' So I went out and started sitting the airport and after that I learned Beaverton. Beaverton has always confused me but, scared as I was, I went out there and I managed to make a living.

"North, northeast, I don't think there's any more [violence] than anywhere else. They've had shootouts in downtown Portland lately. But people are still stuck on 'northeast gang violence.' *Gang violence* is in *south*east. But people would move out *there* in a heartbeat."

Up All Night

Getting through the Night

My principal object being to get through the night, the pursuit of it brought me into sympathetic relations with people who have no other object every night of the year.

Charles Dickens, "Night Walks"

Up All Night

The Mission at Night

At 6:00 p.m. on a Friday night in June they begin lining up on the sidewalk, men of all races and ages, waiting to get into the mission at 526 SE Grand. Many wear multiple shirts and sweaters, even though it's a warm night. The mood of the group is relaxed because it's easy to eyeball the cluster of forty-some people and know that everyone will get in. On nights when more than fifty-five people are in line, the beds are given out by lottery.

Inside, Mike McCoy prepares to greet the homeless when the door opens at 6:30. A year ago, Mike was on the other side of the door, hungry, dirty, and looking for a place to crash. Today, he is one of ten men going through the mission's Recovery Program. He lives in a small hotel room upstairs and shares the work of running the mission at night.

At the end of the day, only one staff person is still around, and he himself is about to go home, leaving Mike and the other "program guys" in charge. In Mark Duhrkoop's view, there is more at stake here than a clean, safe place to sleep. As he puts it, "We are ambassadors to the homeless, helping them to make a choice to change."

In his deep, gravelly voice, Mike McCoy agrees. "We treat the guys as family, with dignity and respect. Because they don't get it anyplace else. And I *know* they don't," he says, "'Cause I didn't get it in the street."

Weather-beaten at age forty-seven, Mike has been clean now for eleven months; he'll graduate from the Recovery Program in two weeks. "Some of these guys out here knew me on the street," he says.

At 6:30, the door is opened and the men start streaming through, each stopping to show a current valid TB card to the man at the door with a clipboard. The cards, required by the larger shelters in town, are proof thhat the bearer has been screened for tuberculosis within the last year.

The men take seats on folding chairs set up on the "chapel" side of the mission, that is, to the right of a partition which runs down the center of the room. Most have been here many times before. They know the routine and they know this room: the linoleum floor in a brick design and propeller fans hanging from the ten-foot ceiling. A simple wooden cross is all there is to look at on the rear wall.

By 6:40 all forty-five men are seated and David, one of the men on program, steps up to the podium. "Any new guys here?" he asks. Even though no one raises a hand, he goes through the rules just the same:

"Please don't line up before six o'clock. We have to cooperate with our neighbors. They're not homeless-friendly. We've already been taken to court about it. So, please, don't come before six.

"Once you sign your name here, you're not to leave the building. Stay in front of the building. We call *'Last cigarette'* about nine.

"If I smell alcohol, or if you're high, I'll ask you to leave. If you have a problem with that, you're out for thirty days. We're all alcoholics or addicts on the program. *We know.* You can't play a player.

"Leave hate, all that street mentality outside. This is the house of the Lord.

"When you go outside to have a cigarette, put your butts in the little can there.

"In the morning, you can have as much coffee as you want, but please bring the cups back inside."

David announces the names of seven men who have mail, but only one person comes forward to claim an envelope.

"Showers for a buck," he says. "There will be no laundry tonight. Please line up."

Eleven men go forward to pay their shower fee. Meanwhile, there are low grumbles of disappointment that they can't get their clothes washed.

When shower sign-up is over, the worship service begins. Tonight's ministry is provided by Pastor Leary and his wife, Judy, from the Tri City Baptist Temple in Gladstone. A guitar player has come with them, a heavy-set man wearing a short-sleeved tropical-print shirt, and *very* white tennis shoes. Without introduction, he begins the service by singing "Jesus Put a Yodel in My Heart."

"Who plays guitar?" the musician asks in his Southern drawl. Three hands go up. "When you play for yourself, that's one thing," he says. "When you start playing for the Lord, I tell you, that's awesome." He gets the men singing "Amazing Grace." In the back row, an old man in black jeans, two wool shirts, his silver hair in a crew cut, knows all the verses. He sings in a bass voice, his hands shaking. The last verse is like a low chant "Praise God, Praise God, Praise God, Praise God …"

His music ministry completed, the guitar player gives a two-minute sermon. "If you can learn to praise God, you'll be okay," he says.

Pastor Leary preaches for five minutes on John 6:40: *"For it is my Father's will that everyone who looks upon the Son and puts his faith in him shall possess eternal life; and I will raise him up on the last day.* God wants to have first place in your heart," the pastor says. He asks the men to bow their head and invites anyone who wants Jesus in his life to raise his hand.

"Come on," the guitar player coaches. "There's somebody *right here* that's got their heart broke."

One man comes swiftly forward and, after a moment, two more follow. Pastor Leary kneels with each one privately, praying in a low voice.

And then the service is over. The last staff person has already gone home. Mike, David, and the other program guys pick up the chairs—the floor will be needed for mattresses—and the homeless men make their way to the other side of the partition to eat.

"We need to go through the rules each and every night because guys have different issues," Mike explains. "Kind of a short-term memory thing." Coming in drunk would be an issue. "Normally what we'll do is we'll ask the gentleman to leave and then come back the next day when he sobers up. If he gets feisty about it, if he gets violent, if he's got a knife on him, we're not to get in fights." Mike figures he's had to call the police maybe half a dozen times in the eleven months he's been here.

The men on program have assigned jobs, running the mission and keeping it clean. "There are two areas that are the backbone—the laundry and the kitchen," Mike points out. "They're the ones that constantly need attention. The sheets and pillowcases are laundered every day, the blankets on a cycle basis. There's quite a bit to do."

He explains that it's not *this* washing machine that's on the fritz, but the one used for personal laundry. "Everything's donation here, and it's not a commercial-grade machine," he says. "You got to make do with what you got." He's pretty sure that Julie Stephenson, the mission staff director, will figure out a way to get the unreliable washer replaced.

Tonight the menu is minestrone soup; the big meal of the day was served at noon. The mission's day program, five days a week from 11:00 to 2:30, offers showers, food, television, and a place to get out of the rain.

By eight o'clock the men have finished eating, and everyone is given a mattress and foam pad. "Everybody kind of settles in."

"At nine o'clock, the night supervisor will go upstairs and the graveyard man will come down. He works till 4:30 in the morning when I relieve him." Mike is technically exempt from taking any shift now that he is this close to graduation and already employed full-time outside the mission, but he elects to take the early morning shift because he wants to stay close to the lives of the homeless.

"It gets pretty quiet at night," Mike says, recalling his own nights on graveyard. "What the guys will do, what at least Dave and I used to do, is we'd bring down all our Bible studies and do our homework. And we'd fold their laundry, get it prepared for them."

Currently, six of the ten men on program share graveyard rotation. "It's tough on recovery," Mike concedes. "There is a certain wear and tear on you doing it. I believe we have a window, anywhere from three months to six, maybe a year, where a guy needs to recover.

"But there always needs to be somebody awake down here," he says. "We've had epileptic seizures, we've had people just wake up having had a bad nightmare, maybe get violent or whatever—we get different things. It can be as simple as wanting water. Usually when I was on graveyard I'd put out a couple pitchers of water for them. We may have guys who are working late. They're on a reserve list and we have to let them in, but they may not come in till say eleven o'clock at night. We normally tell them, 'Just press the buzzer real quick.' If the guy's awake back here, he can still hear it," Mike says with a dry laugh. "The major problem for the night guy is the tendency is to get tired and fall asleep."

Mike believes that doing the night watch put him in touch with the heart of the mission. "I can walk down these aisles and pretty much tell you, probably by name, what's with these guys. We share in their personal lives, their joys, their sorrows, their frustrations, their anger. I actually learn a whole lot more from them than they have any inkling of knowing. A lot of them don't understand what a blessing they are to us. There's nothing that we could possibly do that's too good for any of these guys out here."

At the same time, Mike has learned not to expect too much of these encounters, unless the man is ready to change. "I can give them the tools, I can show them the road. But I can't take them down that road. And nobody could do it for me, either," he says, referring to the five-year period of his life when he was camping out in southeast Portland and using drugs. Like anyone else on drugs, Mike was ready to do anything—except quit using.

He'd actually gone once to Narcotics Anonymous, but he wasn't willing to stop using. "That's the key," Mike says. "My desire wasn't there yet. I needed to go out and do more research, as they say."

Like any other street person, Mike was aware of the Peniel Mission, which had a ninety-four-year history in Portland, but he didn't consider himself someone who went to missions. By preference, he camped out and considered himself a loner.

"But I'd seen a guy that was on this program, that was back out on the street. I got to talking to him, and he said, 'Did you know that there is a *program* there?' I told him, 'Okay, I'll keep that in mind.'"

It wasn't until four or five months later, when Mike had gotten to the point where he was feeling hopeless, that he gave the Peniel program some thought. "It's like one day it dawned on me: I knew I needed to change."

Every mission in Portland has its partisans. Though he'd had no experience of other mission programs, Mike guesses that the success rate at Peniel, Union Gospel, the Salvation Army, or Portland Rescue is "about the same." Some men believe that being located away from the drug dealing on Portland's skid road gave Peniel Mission a bit of an advantage during the last twenty years that it's been on the east side of the Willamette River. "It is a *little* easier to stay clean over here," mission counselor Mark Duhrkoop says cautiously. "The river becomes a barrier."

Some of the guys have been to missions all up and down the West Coast. "*They* say this is the place that they want to be, this is the best one," Mike reports.

Now in its sixth location, the Portland Peniel Mission opened at 247 NW Couch Street, in 1904, as a branch of the head mission in Los Angeles. Founders Theodore Ferguson and his wife Manie had begun preaching on the corner of First and Spring Streets in Los Angeles in 1884, and went on to found the first mission in the city. By the end of 1907, Peniel was in thirty-five locations, including sixteen other towns in California, as well as Portland, Seattle, Alaska, and several cities, most of them seaports, outside the country.

It was Mrs. Ferguson who named it Peniel, a Hebrew word meaning "the face of God," the same word Jacob used to name that place east of the Jordan River, where he wrestled with the angel (Genesis 32:24-32).

Mike believes he was led to Peniel by that man he ran into on the street. "My greatest need at that point was my spiritual need, and I understood that. Not that the others don't have a spiritual program—but I was led *here*," Mike says. "There is a plan and a purpose. I believe that."

Mike took a risk when he came in off the street because he was a wanted felon and could have been sent directly to jail. "I'd been running, I'd been on probation but I wasn't doing my probation reporting. I had two assault charges against me, I had a theft charge, criminal activity and drugs, and I was absconding. I knew that if I came here I would have to turn myself in. My probation officer said, 'Hey, it's admirable that you went and put yourself into this program. But, you know, you still have to deal with all these issues.' I said, 'Fair enough.'

"So while I was going through *this* program, my probation officer sanctioned me to this Day Reporting Center for absconding felons downtown, *and* I also had to go to Providence. That's an outpatient six-month program. I had a full plate, doing all three at the same time. There were times where I'd leave here in the morning and I wouldn't be back till midnight."

Shortly after Mike entered the program, in 1998, Peniel folded, and CityTeam Ministries of San Jose took over the five remaining Peniel missions, all of them on the West Coast. CityTeam's recovery program, like Peniel's, is Bible based.

The mission classes are held four mornings a week, but Mike wasn't able to attend until he'd finished the Multnomah County program. Every weekday for 120 days, he reported in at the Day Reporting Center at nine o'clock in the morning and stayed for three hours of classes. "You call in every night and if your number comes up then you better be prepared," Mike recalls. "They do UA you.

"They want to try and turn people around. Why are people addicted? Why do we have criminal behaviors? It's more or less a secular way of dealing with the issues that those guys have, myself or whoever. We had prostitutes down there, drug addicts. We would cover *criminal thinking distortions*, that's what they called it. Why a person would think the way that they do. They would ask questions like, 'When was the last time you committed a crime?' (The last time I needed drugs.) 'When did your crime stop?' (When I quit doing drugs. Silly me.) That kind of thing. But see it's very basic. It seems so black and white to what they call the normies, the normal people, but yet after living years and years and years of it, it's a comfort zone. Misery can be a comfort zone.

"I was *comfortable* being miserable, but nobody *enjoys* it. It's just we don't know anything else, we're so used to it. We can become like that. And that's what's sad about these guys out here," Mike says, waving a hand toward the mats that are lined up along the mission floor. "I know that they're comfortable being in that state of mind, because I was there."

Mike began in a group of twenty-five at the Day Reporting Center, mixed men and women, and was one of only two who finished. "That's the percentage. They just run. They just aren't going to do it anymore. There's a certain percentage of people that are going to maintain and stay with it, but it's very small. They even *told* me that down there, which puts a little bit of fright in a person. But see, again, it's all in the individual.

"Anyway, I'd come back here, do some chores, do the things I needed to do here, then go back to Providence by six that night. Up *there* you don't fool anybody," Mike says with his distinctive laugh. "Some of the counselors sit there and say, 'I heard something in your conversation that tells me that you might want to go use again.' And I'd be, 'What's that mean?' But you'd pick up after a while, kind of get an inkling. You don't want to learn other people's programs, but you kind of *know* when somebody's going to go use."

In addition to group therapy, which was required at Providence, Mike was invited to choose which classes he wanted to take. He took Anger Management, Communication Skills, How to Be Assertive, and a general education course about drugs, how they affected the spiritual, mental, emotional, physical, and social areas of his life. In that class, he came to an important understanding: "The addiction when I was homeless ran my *whole* life. So therefore my recovery had to be the same. It had to be holistic in the sense that I need to take care of every area of life again.

"It works for me. I'm at the beginning of my journey," Mike says. After a pause, he chuckles. "You know, by no means is there an arrival."

▲

David, who is about to go off duty, calls, "LAST CALL FOR CIGARETTE!" Many of the men are already asleep, but a couple lumber up off their mattresses and trudge outside.

At ten, the lights go out, though there are some smaller reading lights in the rear that the graveyard man can leave on. "At my age now, I can't see very well at night," Mike says, "so I usually used these." But, since he was accustomed to reading a little every night in bed, to read in the dim light in the rear of the mission would put him to sleep. "I would have coffee or go out and stand out in the cold to wake up.

Before he got clean, Mike had been in and out of jail many times. "I mean I'd been abusing drugs for over thirty years," he says. "I had little stints of going to different jails, but never actually convicted of anything. So till about 1995, 1996, I'd basically gotten away with all my crimes that I'd perpetrated for twenty-some years. I used to say I'm either very good or very lucky. And I'd probably figure it's a little of both. But there were times, you know, the drugs *will* get you thrown in jail, number one."

Mike also lost his marriage on account of drugs. "I moved out of there in about '94," he recalls. "She didn't like me using drugs, and I wasn't going to give in. I said, '*This* is *my* sweetheart. See ya.' I was stupid. Using the drug, that's the only thing that counted in my life. And so eventually that became a divorce, and I moved on.

"I had an apartment for a while and then lost that and then I started basically living in a car, dealing dope, running chemicals. I had biker affiliations, and that's how I hooked up with a lot of the heavy methamphetamine users. It's a very violent drug and *they* don't mess around, they don't play with it. They're very different from all of the drug addicts. Very different. Very, very strange. And that's how I ended up on the street.

"Meth will take you down. As a matter of fact, I was just reading an article in *U. S. News* about methamphetamine. It's cheaper than cocaine, gives you more of a rush, and it's also more dangerous than heroin *and* cocaine. Because it mirrors schizophrenia so well. And it can cause permanent brain damage in a person so quickly it's unreal.

"I used to buy from different dealers, I'd make my own. I've done my reactions in hotel rooms, in places where they'd have to send in haz mat afterward if they found out. Because they use about seven different carcinogenics mixed in to get the rush.

"I would shoot it. You can eat it, you can snort it, but shooting it is the way. I would buy twenty dollars' worth, minimum. Usually I'd buy about fifty dollars' worth and shoot it all at once. A half a gram's about fifty bucks. I was up to that, anyway. From fifty to a hundred dollars a day.

"I shared with prostitutes, people I didn't even know. I picked up needles and just used them on the street. I would draw water out of mud puddles to mix it up. I've done all kinds of stupid stuff."

"Self-destruction," he says now. "There was a time where I just felt there was no direction. I didn't care about me, so obviously I didn't care about you or anybody. And that's what leads into crime."

One of the things Mike has learned at the mission is personal accountability. The Bible class uses the *Gospel Echoes* series which was developed in Saskatchewan for inmates. They take actual life situations and solve them from a scriptural basis. As Mike describes it, "It would be the *What would Jesus do?* in a sense. When's the right time to get angry? When we come in, we all deal with basic issues of low self-esteem, addiction, emotional problems, working together as team members. They teach you Bible studies from a practical standpoint."

Mike found a job ten months into the program, and he now spends his days as a warehouseman at Portland Fasteners. "That's basically a nice term for industrial nuts and bolts," he says. "Say somebody's building a highrise downtown: they'll order nuts and bolts for all the girders and stuff. And that's what we do.

"My boss is a great guy to work for. I said, 'Tom, this is where I've been, this is what I've done.' And I was just honest with him. And he says, 'That doesn't even matter.' He says, 'All that counts now is where you're going and what your friends are like now.'"

For the time being, Mike's friends are the homeless guys whom he helps care for. In Mike's view, it's never provider and client: it's always "the guys."

"I get the guys up in the morning. We hit the radio, hit the lights. 'Good morning, guys,' we tell them. 'Coffee's up there.' We usually have sweet rolls out for them. Then we'll go around picking up mattresses. They're usually pretty good about getting out around 5:30. In winter we let them stay till six. But we just can't leave them here all day because we've got to get things going." And Mike, of course, has got to start work at 7:30 at Portland Fasteners.

Mike and his friend Gary will be the first to graduate since CityTeam assumed the management of the mission, and a graduation ceremony is planned for the 29th of June. "Basically I'll get up and talk about this place, give these guys out here the encouragement that they need on a daily basis—sometimes on a minute-to-minute basis."

He welcomes the opportunity to stand up and speak to the men who are still living on the streets. "I know that if I can do it, they can do it," Mike says. "And I want to offer that hope for them. I'm just one beggar showing another beggar where the bread is, and that's a fact."

Up All Night

Georgia's Blues in the Night

It's Thursday night, and veteran disk jockey Georgia Ray sits at the master board, ready to go on air. A big woman with flowing copper-colored hair, she's dressed in purple and wears a small foundry of jewelry—rings, long necklaces, earrings. She has sorted two dozen CDs into five separate piles, positioned tonight's public service announcements on a stand in front of her for easy reading, and dated a fresh KMHD Basic Hour Playlist. She's ready with her headphones on when the red digital numbers on the clock in front of her roll over to 10:00.

"You're listening to KMHD, 89.1, Gresham, owned and operated by Mt. Hood Community College. Jazz with Georgia," she says in her deep throaty voice, and then she plays the first cut of the night, a James Moody tune called "I Can't Get Started." She pushes the gooseneck-mounted microphone away from her face and removes the headphones.

"I *love* to start off with that. It's a long tune, about eight minutes, and it's jazzy, it's bluesy, and it's right up my alley when I'm starting out because at first I have trouble getting it together. You're sitting down and you're cold, but after the first few tunes you start warming up and, oh man, by the time the first hour is over you're in full swing."

Georgia gets her first phone call at 10:05, and she swivels her padded turquoise chair around to answer it. It's some guy calling to say he's glad she's back (she was sick last week) and then he offers the information that he's manic-depressive.

"I have people who call me every week: 'Hey, Georgia, I'm so glad it's you this week.' 'Cause when I miss sometimes, they're very disappointed and they let me know it when I'm back the next week. Boy, do they let me know." Between the radio and the phone, Georgia has developed many relationships which she calls "virtual."

"I get young guys call me on the radio station: 'What did you just *play*? I couldn't believe I heard that.' And I'm going, 'Geez, that's an old one. That's from like 1962 or something.' And they're going, 'God, I haven't heard anything like that before.' And it's like, 'No, and you probably never will again.

But we've got some great stuff coming up.' I get a lot of older people, but when *young ones* call me, God.

"I will admit, from about midnight on, I get some real lulus. I had a man threaten my life because I was playing too much blues. That's just an example of some of the people you get after the bars start emptying out. This man sounded just way over the edge. I mean to threaten a person's life because you're playing too much blues? On the radio? I tell this man, 'Hey, change the channel. Go to bed. Take a shower. Don't talk on the telephone.' Jeez."

She works alone in the small studio; there's no engineer in the next room. To the right of where she sits, stands the FM Modulator, like a big oversized filing cabinet with lights and dials. The station engineers preset it for the volunteer disk jockeys. Georgia calls it the "Don't Touch" machine.

"There is *nobody* here but me. If I have to go to the bathroom, I have to take my chances, let's put it that way. I've been locked out of the studio before, and scared the daylights out of myself, thinking, Oh my God, *dead air*! Dead air's the worst. It's against the law of radio, a total no-no.

"By the way, you're listening to KMHD, 89.1, Gresham. That's right it's Thursday night. I got some old stuff, I got some new stuff, I got some in-between stuff."

As Georgia introduces a 1958 cut by the great tenor stylist, Coleman Hawkins, she asks her listeners, *"What were you doing in the fifties? I remember what I was doing, but I'm not talking."*

She takes off the headphones, sets them aside, and turns down the in-studio volume (controlled separately from the on-air volume). A sign in front of her, above the board, reminds disk jockeys: **Watch Your Levels**.

"Our station is a public broadcasting station, so we don't have the commercials. We do have public spots, community announcements and stuff like that, but we're *music* and we play music. And when they listen to me, they hear even more music, because I don't do a whole lot of talking. I tell them what we're playing, and on we go."

The phone rings and Georgia picks up the receiver. "Just had a birthday, and I'm fifty-one," she says to the caller. They chat for a minute. "Music will haul you through a lot of stuff," she says. "If you're Chicago, you know that." As she hangs up, she says, "I'll be here."

The caller wanted to hear a Stanley Turrentine cut which she doesn't have, though the fabric-covered walls are lined with CDs. She rolls her chair across the room to the shelves behind her, then gets down on all fours on the carpet, inspecting the CDs in the lowest racks. Everything is numbered and indexed in a catalog. She chooses another Turrentine and pulls it off the shelf. "There are five thousand in KMHD's collection," Georgia points out, "counting the blues. Plus another five hundred records." She gets back into the swivel chair and, with the Turrentine in her lap, rolls back to the board. She places the Turrentine CD, *Don't Mess with Mr. T.*, on another CD player and cues it up. Generally, she plays three cuts and then announces the titles.

"I was born outside of Prineville, in a line shack in November. Dad was a dairy farmer, wheat rancher. We were on a large cattle ranch, in one of the line shacks. When a cowboy rides the line, that means he's going way out across the property to pull in all the strays and he stays in a dirt-floored shack on the property line.

"We were snowed in. It was like over the roof at the time. My dad delivered me because we couldn't get out. He said he reached in just like it was a cow and pulled me out. And there I was and here I have been ever since.

"I'm the third sister down which, on a farm, means third in the tub in the kitchen at night, third on the hand-me-down clothes. Third is pretty much piss poor out.

"My family has bounced, since our farm days and I was nine years old, back and forth between southern California and here. Real bouncing. Summers when we were living down there, we would always come up here with my grandparents. First Cascade Locks and then Sweet Home. Cascade Locks is a beautiful place, the storms that whip through there.

"I've got three sisters, and we've got my mom left. Everybody else in the family is pretty much gone. We're all a bunch of squaws. We're French-Indian and Scotch-Irish and we have to contend with alcoholism in our family. Canadian Iroquois means we don't get to collect American money. Canucks is what people call us. Of course we take a little offense to that."

"That's Stanley Turrentine, on tenor sax," she says. *"My name is Georgia and this is your jazz station. Oh yeah, that's the Frank Wess Orchestra, 'Entre Nous.' I think it's time for some Nicholas Payton,"* she says, and she plays one of the young trumpeter's cuts.

"When we moved to California, Dad went to work for Exley Trucking because they're relatives of ours and he worked for the trucking company from there on. We pretty much think he got the cancer from when he was a dairy farmer, cause he got a disease on his hands from the chemicals that he had to deal with back then. They didn't have safeguards like they do now. He died of cancer through his entire body when he was sixty years old."

It's eleven o'clock, and the student AM station next door—kids playing rock & roll—goes off the air. When they close the studio across the hall, Georgia and the security guards will be alone on campus, she in her small studio that locks from the inside, its one long window of bullet-proof glass, and he cruising the vast parking lots in a security vehicle.

A caller wants the name of a song and Georgia tells him it was Charles McPherson on alto sax playing "You're My Thrill" from *Manhattan Transfer.* McPherson played with Monk at the Five Spot in the late fifties.

"Most callers want to know what something was, or to request something. But my rule is I'll only play it if I like it. It's my show."

She's got very decided tastes. Her favorite piano player is Gene Harris, a versatile pianist who's been around since the fifties, when he started out playing soul-jazz with The Three Sounds.

"I don't think my taste has ever changed. It's always going to be a bluesy jazz, a more soulful style. My oldest sister calls it butt-rockin' stuff." Georgia's favorite male singer is Kevin Mahogany. But immediately she adds Kurt Elling. Female, she names Billie Holliday, Ella Fitzgerald. "And, oh, Cleo Laine. A major spectrum of people. Just a huge spectrum. It's just hard to name them all, there's just so many. I love music. Whatever baloney I'm putting myself through—and it's usually self-motivated—it drags me out of it and makes me feel good."

She plays David 'Fathead' Newman, a tenor sax player who worked with Ray Charles for twenty years. "This particular tune," she says, "the first time I heard it I was working at ABC Records, down in California."

Southern California was culture shock for Georgia, who was twelve when her family moved from Biggs Junction, on the Columbia River Gorge, to Norwalk, California.

"Right away, I met the Veloz Brothers: Luis, Charlie, and Kito. Mexican. They were quite a bit older than me and they thought it was really funny, this little hick kid from the country hanging around. They tried drugs out on me before they would take them, and I don't know how many times I woke up on the floor. How I lived through it, I don't know. But back in those days I didn't give a damn."

But it was also in southern California where Georgia seriously discovered music. "My inspiration was my seventh-, eighth-, and ninth-grade glee club teacher, Miss Wilson. She also had a Friday music appreciation class, and she taught us to reach into the music and get what we needed out of it. She'd put on her toe shoes and dance for us, and we were like totally enthralled. I wanted to grow up to be Miss Wilson.

"Way back when I was twelve and thirteen years old, I started going down to Redondo Beach, to Shelly's Manhole, just tons of little tiny spots down there. One of the first musicians I ever went out to see, had to run away from home to do it, was Mose Allison. And then San Francisco, North Beach. I was one of the *original* hippies—but it was actually a beatnik then. God, Mose Allison, Dexter Gordon, Nancy Wilson, *shew*. Errol Garner—just an amazing amount of people. And I think, my God, I got to hear all those people. And now they're gone. That was the West Coast Circuit. Even the clubs are gone.

"Thirty years ago I went to Hollywood. I was going to be the bigshot star. At ABC Records, I was a switchboard operator," she says with a laugh. "I did a little background singing in the studios, and I did a week behind the Righteous Brothers in Las Vegas when I was nineteen. My friend Polly Cutter was having a baby, and she was one of their original four back-up singers. She needed to take a break, 'cause she needed to go give birth. In the recording business you don't give it too much of a break—people forget you too easy. So she had me fill in for that week, and then she came back. It was late in their careers and there was a lot of fighting going on with the Righteous Brothers, right before they broke up that time.

"I started to think that I was going to get to be something, and then I found out that I wasn't *serious*. And you got to be really serious to do it, you got to be real dedicated. And I was screwing off, basically, and ended up just being a working stiff. And also getting laughed offstage because in the sixties I was basically too wasted to sing. Janis Joplin could do it, but she was something else.

"Sometimes I've kind of wondered how I've managed to survive 'cause I was the original wild child. In my youth I went through the entire drug culture. I think I've done everything you could possibly imagine and did as much as I could. I'm the acid queen of the sixties.

"Thank God I don't do any of that anymore, or I probably wouldn't be alive by now." These days Georgia contents herself with sipping Irish Mist and Seven on the rocks, and only when she's out with her sisters.

"*That's David Newman, of course, on sax. Billy Joel wrote that tune. Before that, Carmen. Never have to say* her *name, like Miles, Trane. You're listening to Jazz with Georgia, 89.1, KMHD.*

"About 1975 I came back permanently. That was to bring my son back, who had been born in 1968. We were living in West Hollywood, and he was getting ready to go to school, and I decided it was time to get the H out of there 'cause it was no place to raise a child. And I brought him home, which I consider this place. We came back and I've been here ever since.

"I started in at the station nine years ago 'cause I had read an advertisement in the *Willamette Week* that they wanted volunteers. I'd just gotten split up, things were in a terrible turmoil, if there was anything bluer than me it was grey. I don't know. It was ugly. And I read that ad and immediately reached for the phone and called up Tom Costello—he's the manager of the station—and he said, 'Sure, come on out and give it a shot.'

"I got in the vehicle and came out here. He showed me how to do it once, and said, 'Fly or die.' And that was it: I was on the air. It was like the easiest thing I ever did in my life. Because I'd started out at the recording studio in Los Angeles, I was aware of microphones and the difference they make in sound, and what it *should* sound like. It was almost like it was meant to be."

For the last eleven years, Georgia has worked at Good Samaritan Hospital on the switchboard and as an admitting clerk. She works four ten-hour shifts a week, which gives her Thursday, Friday, and Saturday nights off. "I work Good Sam so I can do the radio stuff. I've had chances to move to other departments and do other things but it would take away my Thursday nights and I can't give up my radio. I love it. It's the only thing, I think, that keeps me sane in this nutty world."

In her late forties she started singing again. "Full circle, here I am starting out, brand new. I haven't done any singing professionally, but I do a lot of karaoke as practice. I'm a triple Scorpio and I'm *real* critical of myself, so that makes it hard to go out in front of other people. If it's not perfect, it tends to piss you off—but I'm trying to get past that. I go out of town, boy, believe me. It's a real struggle for me. It's called 'Coming From a Lifetime of Low Esteem and Knowing Damn Good and Well You're Good and Afraid to Prove It.'"

Georgia describes her style as "blues, jazz, late-night torch singer." Asked to pick three songs which best exemplify that style, she names them without hesitation:

"'I Got a Man.' Lily Wilde is singing that around right now. I love her. So much spirit. 'I Got it Bad and That Ain't Good.' Ella, the way she does it.

"And an old, old, old favorite of mine, from the Mother Earth people way back when Tracy Nelson was the lead singer: 'I'll Never Find Another Man.' It's real low-down torchy stuff. *Real* low-down. I started hearing that when I was sixteen years old, and had my heart broken by my first man. *That* was the first. Not the last." And Georgia laughs as she slips on the headphones.

"'*Teach Me Tonight*,' that's Joey DeFrancesco, an album from 1990. This is James Moody on the jazz station, 'Royal Blue,'" she says. She plays a cut from the saxophonist's *Moody Plays Mancini*.

Georgia describes a show she did two or three weeks back. "I was just rolling from the minute I got here. And my ex was listening for a change. I had spoken to him earlier that day and he said he would be listening, and I was feeling a little self-conscious 'cause he doesn't listen as a rule. He's not into music at all; he couldn't sing if you paid him. But, yeah, I'm a sucker. I still love him."

At KMHD, disk jockeys are only expected to stay until 1:00 am. The station purchases five hours of feed from KLON-FM, a California jazz station at Long Beach State, which airs from 1:00 to 6:00 a.m. "I really do think they got the very best thing they could find on the West Coast," Georgia says. "They're great."

But Georgia often keeps her show going until two. "A lot of times I'm getting my second wind. At one I stop and think about it: No, I got more stuff to play, I can't stop now. But you never know. Sometimes when I look at it I'll go, Oh, God, I'm just tired, I'm going home."

Tonight she's decided to stay. She plays Jack Teagarden's "Mis'ry and the Blues," from *The Jazz Club Vocals*, a CD that is no longer available.

"*They used to say Jack was one of the few white men that can sing the blues,*" she says on air. Teagarden's voice is gruff and authentic, and he accompanies himself with a silky dirge-like trombone:

> *Blues in the morning*
> *Mis'ry in the evening*
> *Keep me wondering what I ought to do.*
> *Almost out of money*
> *Guess you think that's funny,*
> *Even though you know I'm still in love with you.*

"*This is Georgia,*" she says, "*and I'm going to be around for a while.*"

Up All Night
Lullaby

If the pop singer Madonna were a nurse, she would be Kerry Cawrse. Glamorous and shapely, with blunt-cut peroxide hair, grey blue eyes, and clipped rapid speech, Kerry, twenty-nine, is the night shift charge nurse on Ten North, the oncology ward at Doernbecher Children's Hospital.

A big fish mobile dangles above the nursing station where Kerry is headquartered with four other nurses and two certified nursing aides, all wearing brightly colored scrubs.

On a night in August, a small sleepless boy wearing a paper breathing mask pedals a green John Deere tricycle. His mother follows behind, pushing the rolling IV pole on which hangs a cowboy hat and a small stuffed monkey. They cut a sharp corner around the front of the nursing station and head back down the other corridor.

"It's all kids getting bone marrow transplants or receiving chemotherapy, that's it," Kerry explains. "There's no other patients. Some patients stay three to five days if they're on chemotherapy. I would say four months is a pretty average bone marrow transplant stay with no complications. Some leave at three, but a lot stay till nine, so …" Often Kerry doesn't finish her sentences; a rush of words and feelings tumble toward a final *"so …"*

Doernbecher has only been doing bone marrow transplants since May 1998. "Before that we were just straight oncology. We sent our bone marrow transplants to Seattle to the Hutch or to Children's in San Francisco."

With the new bone marrow transplants, she notes, not only did the average stay jump hugely, but the nurses now have patients who are much harder to take care of.

Acute lymphoblastic leukemia, or ALL, is the most common form of childhood cancer, usually striking between the ages of two and ten. About twenty-five hundred children are diagnosed each year in the U.S. The treatment is chemotherapy until complete remission is achieved. A bone marrow transplant is actually a transfusion of bone marrow cells used as a "rescue" for the patient after chemotherapy, an option for very high-risk cases or following relapse. Between the two protocols, the cure rate is now up around 80 percent.

"A lot of them die, though," Kerry says. "I'm not sure what percentage. It depends on what kind of transplant. When we first started, all of our kids lived because we did just sibling related, we did just *perfect* matches of siblings, and we did that for three or four months. Now we're doing matches that are five out of six unrelated, four out of six unrelated, so …

"I cry when someone relapses. I mean I really do *invest* myself in these little people, and that's what makes me good, I feel. But that's also why I don't want to do it forever, because it is very draining. I mean, you get tired of going to funerals, you get tired of the phone ringing."

Kerry's phone rings because she gives her home number out to patients and their families. Not all nurses do that.

"We try to make assignments based on acuity; we rate them on a scale of one to six, on how busy they are and how many nursing hours they take. So like if you have one bone marrow transplant patient, the other two are probably going to be simpler diagnoses. We also assign differently according to what day in or out of the transplant they are, 'cause they're busier at certain times than others.

"I call them my little bald kids," Kerry says. "You *know*, when they walk in the door, you're going to know these people for a long, long time.

"I always tell everyone that normal kids don't get cancer. I don't know if it's the cancer, but they're much more adult-like. I mean I've heard eight-year-olds and six-year-olds say things that are far wiser than anything an adult would ever say. They don't get angry like adults do; they don't feel cheated; they don't get bitter. Adults with a terminal illness, in my experience, are bitter, hateful, bossy—they're so angry. Kids, they are not like that. They play, they're still very much just kids.

"They're very wise for their age. I've heard many kids ask their parents, 'Are you ready?' Because they get to a point where they *know* it's time. And they're much more worried about Mom and Dad than they are themselves.

"I mean the families are very courageous also; they have to be. But the kids are *really* amazing little people."

Kerry becomes well acquainted with these families, because they, too, live here at Doernbecher. This is family-centered care. Each of the sixteen hospital rooms on this floor has its own private bath with shower. Besides the patient's bed, each has a daybed window seat and a sleeper chair, accommodating two adults sleeping over.

"We bring in movies for the kids, stuff like that. That's what makes it fun. I lie in bed and read a book to them if I have time. Or if Mom needs to go for a walk or do laundry."

The laundry room, along with a kitchen in which parents can make snacks, are right here on Ten North. There's also a playroom with easels, crayons, work tables, and padded benches, a huge roll of butcher paper mounted on the wall, plastic cars, puzzles, and trays of baseball cards. There's a dollhouse and an aquarium, and shelves stuffed with games—chess, checkers, Adventure Park, Clue, Scrabble, Sorry, Yahtzee. Beguiling titles spill from bookshelves: *The Snowy Day, Camel Caravan,* Mi Primer Gran Libro Práctico, *Abraham Lincoln, Brer Rabbit and His Friends,* not to mention the intriguing title, *Where, Oh, Where's My Underwear?*

Unless their ANC (absolute neutrophil count) is 500 or greater, however, the children can't leave their room. And the blood count is just one indicator. Besides the fevers and the low neutrophil count, transplant patients are vulnerable to graft-versus-host disease. Some kids are knocked out by it, and the chemotherapy itself can cause nausea, anemia, and fatigue.

▲

Kerry is not one who chose night shift: for her, nights have been the required rite of passage in a new career.

"Everything about night shift is fine except for the way you feel," she says. "I mean you've got to figure out how to get five or six hours of sleep. You've got to turn your phone off, you can't leave it on for emergencies. I'm like, if it's actually an emergency everyone knows I'm asleep and they will send the neighbor, somebody to beat on the door. I mean basically you've just got to figure out how to get as much sleep during the day as you can. I have blackout shades, I have fans.

"I get home at 7:30, I go right to bed. Some people don't. Some people eat breakfast, but I don't. I don't talk on the phone, nothing. 'Cause I find if I do anything that gets me going, then I don't get enough sleep. I go basically right to bed, so …

"I'm home by myself during the day 'cause my sister works. And on weekends, when she's home and I've worked, she watches the TV on like *mute.* I mean like she *knows.*"

Still, Kerry had a hard time changing her internal clock in order to sleep days and stay alert nights.

"The first eight months to a year I was miserable. I would sometimes want to cry before I had to go to work 'cause I just hated it. Now I don't feel that way; now I know how I expect to feel and I'm used to feeling that way and I've learned how to function feeling that way. But for the first eight months it was awful. If I had kids or something, I can't even imagine. I mean I just can't imagine.

"But we do have more fun on nights. Most of us aren't married. Some are, but they tend to be a younger, more flexible group of people. Where like day shift, things like holidays and weekends off are a *very* big deal. On nights it's never like that. It's like, 'You want the weekend off? I'll work this weekend, I don't care.' They tend to be more easy going.

"But I gained like twelve pounds. People bring potato bar, nacho bar, you know. It's munchy food. People have cookies, Snickers Bars out of the thing, popcorn, it's like, it's grazing food. That's why so many night nurses are overweight, 'cause you do, you graze all night long.

"It's a slower pace at night," Kerry observes. "All the patients go to sleep, there's no management. You have like half as many people, no doctors. I mean the only time there are doctors is if you call them to come. There's no physical therapy, occupational therapy, x-ray, none of that stuff.

"During the day, say there was a crisis situation, a pediatric attending physician would make all the decisions. Well, at night there's no one but you, so you make all the decisions till someone else gets here that is better qualified. You get to do that more on your own—it's a little bit more challenging. That would probably be the one thing I like."

Raised in Eastern Oregon, Kerry attended University of Portland, thinking she would be a teacher. "Basically, I went to college for six years. I completed almost my fourth year of elementary education, did my student teaching in a fifth-grade classroom over in Portland Public Schools, and I hated it. So, of course, I called my dad: 'I hate this, I don't want to do it. I have three months left and I can't stand it.'

"So he says, 'Well, what do you want to do?' and I go, 'I don't know.' My best friend had gone into nursing right when we got out of high school. And I thought, you know, she has lots of time off, she makes enough money, she's not rich by any means but she doesn't have to work *all* the time, she seems to like it: I'll just do that.

"There's tons of different things you can do. There's travel nursing if you want to do that, you can work in schools, you can work for insurance companies, you can sell things for medical supply companies, you can do day surgery, you can work for a Lake Oswego pediatrician and look in well kids' ears. So I thought that would give me a lot more options. I knew I needed to finish *something*: I'd been in school for a long time. So I said, 'Well, I might try nursing school,' and I did and I ended up liking it, so ..."

In 1995, Kerry graduated from University of Portland with a bachelor's in nursing.

"After I did all my clinical rotations, I liked pediatrics the best. One of my instructors was really good friends with the nurse manager at Doernbecher, and she got me an interview with her. She gave me the job, and ever since then I've just stayed."

Working 75 percent time, on her fourth year, she made $42,000 in 1998. "I would think if you were willing to work full-time," she says, "I mean you could make sixty, I would say, easily. But that's working full-time. That's working a lot." Kerry finds the work so emotionally intense that she can only manage three-quarters time.

"I remember one little boy I took care of, he died. His mom and I had become friends. A year later the phone rings in the middle of the night and my sister comes into my room and she says, 'So and so's on the phone.' And I thought, Gosh, has it been a year? 'Cause a lot of times they'll call me around that time. But it was that her husband had died. And it was me she wanted to talk to. It's an automatic trust they have with you, because they have to trust you with *so much*, right away.

"I had another patient who was from Alaska. His mom comes by every year within a good month of when he died. Every time she calls, and every time I meet her at the same place. We don't do anything but look at the scrapbook that he had—we talk about *it* for an hour. The rest of the year, I get postcards saying, 'We're here, we're there.' But it's like once a year, for the last three years, she calls. And I call her, too. And I would do that as long as she needs me to.

"Some people don't do that stuff. I don't know how to *not* do it," she says.

For Kerry, the only way not to do it is to leave Ten North altogether and, reluctantly, she recently made that decision.

"I have given my notice," she explains. "I took a job in the intensive care unit, for that reason. I mean I *love* the kids and it's been fun for four and a half years, but you don't leave it at work. You've taken care of these people— I see them more than I see my own parents. So then when one of them dies or there's a problem it's *much, much harder*, because you know the dog, you know all their family, they tell you *everything*."

There's an eloquent photo collage hanging in the corridor of Ten North: snapshots of kids in cribs, kids with lesions, and kids who look like sleek young princes. There are tiny frail kids, kids with huge eyes, kids in the snow, kids hooked up to IVs, and kids in wheelchairs. Kids hug siblings, hold puppies, blow out birthday candles, and clutch baby bottles. They wear big t-shirts, cowboy hats, face paint, eyeglasses, or respirators. One little bald boy examines a policeman's handcuffs. Most of the kids are smiling.

At the nursing station, her colleagues talk quietly. "Sara's blood sugar is down. I'm so excited," one nurse says. The second nurse, in a penguin-spotted shirt and fuchsia cotton drawstring trousers, points out. "Well, it helps that she's up and walking."

Night shift has a rhythm here: the beginning of the shift is relatively lively, it goes dead after midnight, and then picks up again toward morning. "I would say 3:00 like to 5:30 is the worst time," Kerry says. "What I've discovered happens in the morning is the lights come on, new stimulus starts happening, new people are coming in, you kind of get that second wind. I'm fine when it gets 7:30, I'm like awake again. But three o'clock in the morning is awful, awful."

Each staff member is entitled to an hour break, and Kerry takes hers between three and four o'clock. She goes into the staff lounge, turns out the lights, and stretches out on a couch.

Then, in the hours just before dawn, Kerry goes silently from room to room on a meds round. In one room, a young mother is awake. She sits in the window seat, a blanket wrapped around her shoulders, staring at the city twinkling far below.

Kerry checks the IV level of the sleeping child, then moves to the window seat, where she whispers a greeting. Through the window they can see thousands of households. Kerry imagines the young mother is thinking they all have healthy children, tucked snugly into their beds. Hospital machinery purrs softly, accentuating the silence. Kerry stands for a moment in the dark, her hand resting on the woman's shoulder, offering what comfort she can.

Up All Night

Obdulia at the Rose Garden

Traffic is stop-and-go on NE Broadway as people pour out of the huge sports arena. Every lane is jammed and the dark street glows red with brake lights. Crowds of pedestrians jaywalk between the cars, swarming to distant side streets where the parking is free. As traffic lurches forward, carrying away the exhilarated spectators, another group of people quietly enters the Rose Garden and goes to work. These are the janitors, and all thirty of them are from Mexico.

One of them is Obdulia, a dark petite woman, twenty-three, with childlike hands and a voice that rarely rises above a whisper. She speaks Spanish, the language her parents share, though her father's first language is *cholcolteco*, a Mixtec dialect.

She doesn't know English, but working here at the sports arena, she has learned to recognize *Portland Trail Blazers* (*basquetbol*) and *Winterhawks* (*hockey*). In March, *el cantante* Billy Joel sang here. The concrete floor of the arena was *helado* for "Disney on Ice." Sometimes they bring *tierra* into the arena. Afterwards, big machines go through, scooping it all back up.

"I know they use the dirt for some kind of truck races," Obdulia says in Spanish, "but I don't know what they call them. They don't let us in to see them."

Obdulia does not attend any of the events. The tickets are expensive.

Tonight, as always, she is sleepy when she begins her shift. She's had only three hours of sleep and she feels the exhaustion in her feet, her back, her shoulders, her eyes. How easy it would be to just collapse on the floor, curl up in a quiet corner and go to sleep. But no. Her unit of eight workers is assigned the fourth floor, where they will clean *las oficinas*, as Obdulia calls them. She does not understand the purpose of seventy private rooms in an entertainment complex, but she does not ask questions. Each of these rooms has a wet bar and a private bath with television. A glass wall permits a view of the arena, and on the other side of the glass there are twelve seats in a private box. Obdulia begins by picking up the trash that litters the bar, counter top, and coffee table, and putting it in a big bag of clear plastic.

"It is very hard because they call us in to work different schedules every day. Sometimes they call us to go in at eleven at night. They let us know two hours beforehand. *Es muy difícil.* Sometimes they won't find me at home. Sometimes I have to run to leave off my son and get myself to work."

Her son, Oscar, is a healthy, pudgy two-year-old.

"He stays with the *señora*—I have to get all his food together—and I get him in the morning. I pay her ten dollars each time I leave him. I earn $6.50 an hour.

"Night work, they pay us once a month. I get about nine hundred dollars. I work with my sister as well, cleaning houses with her during the day. Even with the two arenas, the work isn't every night. There are some nights when I clean the arenas after I've cleaned houses all day.

"My friend, Susy, first brought me into this work. She went and put in an application, and they called her. She took me in and showed me how to apply and we just stayed on and worked.

"The houses are through my sister. She met some woman and told her she'd clean her house, and then met some of her friends. My sister speaks English and does the driving, buys the cleaning supplies, everything. So she gets most of the money and pays me *el mínimo.*"

Cleaning houses, Obdulia works Tuesday through Saturday. "On Monday, I shop and wash. I've learned to use the buses. The laundromat is *lejos,* almost to the other Fred Meyer, up on Lombard.

"With the night work, it is hard sleeping in the daytime. Sometimes I arrive home at eight, seven, six in the morning. Then I have to go pick up Oscar. I come home and I can't get to sleep because of my son. I can't sleep with him running around. I can't leave him with the *señora* because I'd have to pay for that day, too."

When they are permitted a small break, Obdulia goes outside for a moment to see if the cold air won't wake her up. She stands on a concrete fourth-floor terrace, the outdoor smoking area for this floor, and looks out into the dark. Unlike her village, where there is always plenty to see in the sky, there are never many stars here in Portland. Obdulia grew up in the Mixteca, the rugged Oaxacan countryside where people live in small, scattered settlements. There her family struggled to grow subsistence crops in impoverished or eroded *tierra.*

"Oscar was born here, so he is *un ciudadano.* The truth is, I have no idea if I can become one. I wouldn't want to be turned down, but, sure, I'd like to be legal.

"It's difficult to work without papers. There's no problem cleaning houses because we don't work through a company. But the night work, that's through a company. All of us on staff have our so-called 'social security.'"

But because the social security numbers are not valid, people in Obdulia's situation cannot open a bank account.

"Sometimes when you go to rent an apartment they ask for a social security card. Even for an apartment! *No es fácil.*" Obdulia currently pays $475 a month for a small one-bedroom in north Portland. "*La verdad es*, I can barely pay the rent and living expenses," she says.

As she and Susy are letting themselves into yet another suite, Obdulia is told by her unit leader that they will be sent down to the arena, where they are short of help tonight. They take the elevator to the first floor and check in with the supervisor of that unit, a young man from a small town in Guerrero. He dispatches Obdulia to the top of the bleachers, and she makes the wearying ascent.

In the high reaches of the bleachers, she turns to look out over the catwalk and platform suspended 105 feet above the arena floor. From steel trusses hang wires, cables, metal bars, hinges, platforms, great chrome brackets and braces. But tonight, Obdulia sees something else has been added—rings, ladders, ropes, trapezes, harnesses, and nets dangle high in the night. Below, in one corner, she makes out the silent bandstand with its painted gold facade.

She stoops to pick up straws, popcorn, boxes, candy wrappers, and colorful candies—*popotes, palomitas, cajas, papeles de dulces, y dulces de muchos colores.* The floors are concrete, and the red cloth seats snap closed— unless they are broken. First the trash, then sweeping with a short-handled black broom.

"I would like to work with people who speak English because I never have. I could practice speaking. In Mexico, I had just six years of schooling, *básica*, and they didn't teach me much.

"For Oscar there are a lot of opportunities. Here one doesn't pay for school. I would work so he could study. I think he can go when he's four. I don't know much about it, but I can ask when I go to *la clínica.*

"What luck that Oscar has never been sick, because otherwise I wouldn't be able to work. He helps me a lot by not getting sick."

She kneels down to scrape up a wad of chewing gum that has been ground into the floor. The broom, which she leaned against a seat, slides to the floor.

"In Mexico, I came from a ranch, a small village, without light in the streets, with small houses there. Nochixtlán is maybe three hours away and it's larger.

"In the village, there are like maybe fifty or seventy houses, but all very spread out. There are ranches, trees, mountains. We raise *maiz, frijoles*, wheat, potatoes, and that's about it. String beans, but only when it rains. I grew up there, and my mother is still there." She is hit with a strong sense of her mother. She could be home with her mother in Mexico. Sometimes she thinks that's what she wants. "But not to be married. Anyway, I don't think so. Maybe it would just be more work."

When Obdulia was sixteen, she moved to Mexico City, where an older sister was already living with her husband. "I went with them to work because there's no work in the village," she says, "nor in Nochixtlán either." In the city, she worked for five years as a domestic.

"I would start at six in the morning by washing the cars. I'd feed the dog, then start cleaning and dusting. I prepared meals, made beds, and washed. It was the same routine every day. I worked until eight at night and I had my own bedroom. On Saturday and Sunday, I went to the house of my sister. They lived on the outskirts of the city, toward San Pedro, in the north.

"In Mexico there's a lot of work, but they don't pay anything," Obdulia observes. She was frustrated because she couldn't earn enough to help her parents.

"I had a sister who'd been living in the United States for five years. She came home to visit Mexico. She wanted the family to come to Portland with her. She said there was work.

"I wanted to come, but the journey frightened me. I came alone with my cousin, Leticia. It was expensive and it was dangerous, being two women crossing. *Está muy feo el camino*. We came through Tijuana. Really bad.

"We were ten people walking in the night. In the day we hid under bushes. It was eight days crossing *El Cerro de las Águilas*. One whole day we had nothing to eat. The *coyote* was a kind man, but the journey was scary because of *la migra*. I was used to walking in the hills at home so I wasn't afraid of animals. I was afraid only of the border patrol."

Although she didn't know it, Obdulia was one month pregnant when she came across. She had gone home to her village to say goodbye to her parents and an old boyfriend. "That's when I got pregnant with Oscar.

"In Portland, I gave birth at the hospital on the hill. I told the father on the telephone, but he didn't want to come. So now my thinking is that he just won't have anything of Oscar. When Oscar turns eighteen, I'll tell him who his father is, but for now, no. *Eso es mi idea*.

"Anyway, I arrived in Portland in January of 1997 and began working that same month. I worked in the country in a *nursería*. It was small potted trees, fruit or flowering trees. I didn't care for it but I stayed with it because *necesité el dinero.*"

Needing the money, she worked until she was eight months pregnant, then quit the nursery and went to work cleaning houses with her sister until she delivered. After she had Oscar, the family made it possible for her to take four months off. "Then I went back to work with my sister."

Break time. Obdulia leaves her cleaning supplies and goes to the event level floor, where she retrieves her lunch from a blue plastic locker. In the employee break room, she doesn't spot Susy, and so she sits at a long metal table with a group of girls from Michoacán. They are talking about how they must be careful when they are using *los líquidos* because some have fumes and some are not supposed to touch the skin. Obdulia remembers how confused she was when she first saw at the grocery store all the chemicals available for cleaning.

"I had a lot to learn. In a lot of *las casas* we had to use different products on different types of furniture, in order not to damage them. Now I've learned to read the names on the labels."

She unwraps cold *tortillas* and eats them with *frijoles*. She has one piece of chicken, and she saves it for last. When lunch break is over, she stuffs the empty plastic bag into her jacket pocket. She can use it again tomorrow. She has heard that they have only *dos horas más* to clean, and she hopes that it's true. She's sent now to mop around the red arena seats with a string mop and an industrial mop bucket on wheels.

Trudging back to the upper level, she realizes eating has made her feel even sleepier. She fights the temptation to sit down on one of the cloth-covered seats. For just a moment, she closes her eyes. Opening them again, she sees the trappings of the circus far below. She saw a circus once in Mexico. She would like to bring Oscar to see one. She pictures his black eyes wide, sees him tossing up his hands in delight.

Amidst great sweeps of violet and silver light, an elegant black man wearing a top hat revolves on a high platform in el centro. *He is singing, and the music pounds dramatically. Gold sequins cover the lapels of his white tuxedo and spangle his coat, vest, and hat.*

A black mare trots jauntily in a circle with her head down. Her flowing tail as thick and shiny as Obdulia's grandmother's hair. A yellow-haired man rides her plump broad back, tossing balls into el aire.

Six white stallions, their black bridles studded with jewels, prance in formation, white plumes waving above their heads and shoulders. A tall, slim woman in a gown of powder blue cracks un látigo *over them, and they canter in a line, CRACK, now reverse, CRACK, now run in pairs, CRACK, now six abreast and, for a grand finale, CRACK, stand up on their hind legs, walk forward and take a bow, as her whip swirls above their nervous backs.*

Strobes of saffron, rose, and tangerine illuminate the wires high above the arena floor, where handsome white-toothed men in satin pantalones *are poised tense and ready, like constellations yet to be named.*

Far below, in the shadows, big cats pace their cages, waiting in the dark. Metal doors slam open and shut, and the solid flanks of Bengal tigers leap into the light of the center ring. White-throated, los tigres *yawn, preen, snarl, and bare their teeth.*

Fourteen velvet elefantes *with drowsy, bruised eyes turn circles on pedestals and then do headstands, their wrinkled flesh falling forward. Draped in gold and white tapestry, they line up by size, front feet positioned on the back of the larger elephant in front. For a finale, they trot in a linked chain, trunk to tail. Behind one small elephant, a clown runs with shovel and scooper.*

Los deshechos de los elefantes, Obdulia laughs to think. Glad that she doesn't have to clean that up, she goes back to her mopping, back to her other dreams.

"When I'm thirty, *si Dios quiere,* I'll speak English, and learn to drive, and have a good job. I'll clean several houses, or work with another company where it's easier. As Oscar gets a little older, maybe he'll settle down a little and I can devote myself to getting more things done."

It's quarter to five when the janitors finish cleaning the Rose Garden. They bring the *escobas* and *recogedores* to the maintenance office where they'll be stowed away until the next night.

Outside, the air is fresh. Her friend, Susy, drives Obdulia back to her neighborhood in north Portland, letting her off at the apartment of the *señora,* only a block from where Obdulia lives.

The woman lets her in, and Obdulia can smell coffee. She stands over the couch where her son sleeps and, without her saying a word, he opens his eyes. Seeing his mother, he tosses up his hands in delight, his black eyes wide.

Up All Night

While the Weary World Is Sleeping

While the moon her watch is keeping
All through the night
While the weary world is sleeping
All through the night

"All Through the Night"
Welsh traditional

Up All Night

Street Sweeper

On the east bank of the Willamette River a warehouse serves as office, shop, and garage for the City's Bureau of Maintenance. At 9:45 on a July evening, the night is not yet black at the windows, but a rich blue. Cafeteria tables and metal chairs ring the room, leaving a huge space in the center for the twenty-two men and women lying on exercise mats. Coached by a trainer from High Tech Sports Therapy, these people are working through their nightly exercise regimen. The bureau provides this program to protect the street-cleaning crew against the physical stresses of their job.

Terry Wade, a delicate woman with fine cheekbones and beautiful skin, has finished her fifty push-ups and has begun stretching. Five years ago, at forty-three, Terry became the City's first female sweeper driver and is still the only woman driving night shift.

When everyone gets to their feet, they have ten minutes to collect their gear. The night operations supervisor, Willie Washington, gives announcements, then dispatches the crews, who head out of the warehouse toward the big yard where their vehicles are parked under the massive supports for the Fremont Bridge. There they'll prepare, or "pre-trip," the water tankers, dump trucks, and street sweepers that they use each night to clean the city streets. For Terry, this means filling her sweeper with water and making sure the brushes are as long as a dollar bill. If not, new brushes are in order.

Workers service a route in this order: first the "flusher," driving a water tanker, lays down a half-lane-wide swath of water. The "buncher" follows in a six-yard dump truck, which he (or she) parks at intervals. Using a shovel for cutting grass and weeds and a broom for unplugging the catch basins, he sweeps debris into the path of the oncoming sweeper. If something is too big for the sweeper to pick up, the buncher shovels it into his or her own truck. Terry comes last, driving an Elgin Pelican, which cost ninety-six thousand dollars new two years ago. It carries one hundred sixty gallons of water and will hold thirty gallons of diesel.

If the buncher comes across something that the sweeper won't pick up, such as a 2x4, a piece of pipe, a hubcap, a rock ("larger than a fist" the buncher's instructions say), large pieces of cardboard, or a tree limb, the object is supposed to be shoveled directly into the dump truck.

"We don't pick up dead animals very well," Terry points out. "Instead we drag them along, and they stink and they get the fur beat off them. So we always like the buncher to pick them up ahead of time." She gives a wry laugh. "You know, for a joke they like cover them up."

Since Terry is not always assigned bunchers *and* flushers, she is grateful to have both tonight.

Each sweeper driver has an unvarying route, though it takes many nights to complete. Her flusher and buncher confer with Terry to make sure they know where she's going tonight. She is headed toward the corner of Interstate and Going, in the midst of Route 3, Map 6, where she left off last night. Wally will flush for her; Mike will bunch. Yes, they know this route, which will take them to Swan Island. But just in case, they both have a copy of the big Night Operations Inventory, a book full of plastic-encased maps of the sixty-five areas that are swept at night. Most maps are named after an arterial, like Interstate, McLoughlin, or Terwilliger, though a few of them have been given colorful nicknames by the sweepers. Short Wino is what they call the shorter of the two skid road routes, and Rat Race is what they call downtown.

It's 10:55 when Terry leaves the Stanton Yard; the flusher and buncher have already gotten a thirty-minute jump on her. The sweeper travels fifteen or twenty miles an hour, and it takes Terry eight minutes to reach Interstate and Going where she first drops her broom. Sure enough, there's a swath of water half the width of the far right lane, and that's where she begins to sweep. She meets Wally, her flusher, at the corner; he's about ready to head back and refill.

The Elgin's brushes do two different jobs. The two curb brooms circle in toward the center; the main broom, which stretches all the way across the back, rolls the opposite direction as the pilot wheels, kicking the debris onto the elevator (the conveyor belt), which carries it up to the hopper.

Terry "drives right, sweeps right": that is, she sits on the right side of the cab, sweeping the right curb, steering with her left hand on the knob, her right hand in the window. Her left buttock is elevated up off the seat and she's leaning out the right window so she can see her own curb brushes. A protruding metal cage protects her head when she leans out the window.

The smell of dirt and diesel fills the cab as she bounces along to the sweeper's high-pitched whine. The sweeper has three-point balance: two big tires in front, and two little pilot wheels close together in back. Like a military jeep in rough terrain, it gives a bumpy ride.

The hopper on Terry's Elgin will handle four cubic yards before it needs to be emptied. In summer, that's only once a night, but in fall it quickly fills with leaves, in winter with sand and gravel. To Terry, during those seasons, it feels like "you're dumping all night."

Terry started with the Maintenance Department in August of 1992. "I got hired as a laborer, and I decided to go to nights because I thought other people might *not* want to go to nights," she says bluntly. As a laborer, she was working streets in the core district downtown.

"Laborers are on foot. They have the hose and they squirt all this stuff out from the curb so the sweepers can get them later. Now, the flushers help retract the hose, but when I did it they stretched out the hose and then you're dragging the hose and it was really hard. I thought, I'm too old for this.

"I was a laborer for probably close to a year, ten or eleven months, and then I became a utility worker, involved with emptying the garbage cans that are on the mall downtown. I did that for about four or five months, and they had some internal stuff happen at the Maintenance Bureau and two sweeper drivers on nights were let go. I was really lucky because they just put me in one of those people's jobs. They said, 'Well, it's yours.'

"I had a lot of training because when I bunched they would often put me with this fellow, Frank, who was close to retiring. He taught me how to drive the sweeper. I was really intimidated. I hadn't been around equipment, I hadn't driven tractors; in fact, machinery was my nemesis." As Terry points out, she does not even particularly like driving a car.

Street sweeping takes a lot of concentration. "A lot more than it looks like because whichever curb broom is next to the curb"—she lays her hands side by side—"like this is a curb and this is a curb broom, you want it right *here*. You don't want it up *here*, you know. You always want to keep it lined up. It's kind of hand-eye coordination 'cause the sweepers, they've got big gears off these two little pilot wheels in back and so it's like driving a bumper car kind of.

"You can't hold the steering so you palm it. You kind of line things up. The machine is so big, I think it's nine feet wide. So it's really hard.

"The ones that we have now are automatic. They're hydrostat: they run on hydraulic fluid, rather than gears, and reverse is in the gas pedal. You go forward and then you push on the end of the pedal and it will go backwards, though when you're in really heavy machinery you don't back up very much 'cause you can't see all the way behind you. But if I'm sweeping and I go through a particularly heavy spot and I kind of glance down and I can see I didn't get it all, sometimes I think it's just as easy to back up a little bit and then use the back draft for picking up, kind of *scraping* the dirt up. And then go forward again.

"Some of the guys say, 'Any knucklehead can do it.' But I didn't feel that way. Frank would say, 'Okay, I'm going to walk along. You just try to make a straight line.' When we'd look back, he'd say, 'Looks like a snake's been here.'" Terry laughs to recall Frank's teasing. "But he was really good," she adds.

Tonight, following Map 6, Terry takes Going to Swan Island, and works her way through the industrial park. She sweeps past the Coast Guard at Mock's Landing, Federal Express, McDonald's (still open), Peterbilt, the Fred Meyer Dairy Plant, the Drop Anchor Café, Northwest Box Manufacturing, Bingham Co. at 3014 N Wygant, Freightliner, Office Depot, Mohawk Industries on N Basin, Oregon Transfer, Walter E. Nelson on N Tomahawk Island Drive, Budweiser, and Dahlin/Fernandez/Fritz on N Cutter Drive.

"When Freightliner changes shift, maybe around twelve, it's easier to just pull over and let the traffic abate, because they drive like crazy," Terry says. "Everybody's racing in and out." But most of the time, the streets are empty and the sweeping hypnotic. She listens to Art Bell on the radio.

"For me, a good night is a route I really like and everything running pretty smoothly. You may be kind of edgy before you come to work, but then you start sweeping and you just get really *engrossed*. You're making pretty good time and you're just kind of cruising. And then you look, and, gosh, it's 12:30!

"They like you to get twenty-five, twenty-seven miles a night. That means in theory you should probably try to get at least twelve before lunch and then kick it up. Sometimes it's really easy to do and it seems like you're just flying.

"And then there are other times you just go a lot slower. Sometimes the machine trails, and you fiddle with the brooms and you adjust and you've still got like a little trail that goes back and then you double back, trying to get it, get that little extra bit, and all you do is add to it. That just makes you grind your teeth. A bad night it's just little things go wrong.

"Like once I had some asshole out at St. Johns pull out of the Wishing Well and it didn't dawn on me. I felt this *bump* and I kind of lurched once and I thought, Oh my goodness. So I hit the brakes more and I got lurched two other times and then he drove off. He was drunk and he turned the wrong way. You know it didn't hurt the sweeper; they're like tanks."

Eventually, every street in Portland gets cleaned. Downtown is cleaned every night; residential streets are cleaned during the day, when the Maintenance Department is able to advise residents that they should move their cars before the sweepers come through. "Nights we do arterials and the streets where the traffic would be too heavy to get during the day.

"From MLK I go down Lombard, I take a little divot off of Vancouver, I go down a block off of Peninsula, I go down a block one way on Portsmouth, I go all the way to the University of Portland. It's not like a grid. Some of the sweeper drivers have a lot more grids on their maps.

"As far away as I go would be Jantzen Beach or St. Johns. I go as far south as Weidler." "I love sweeping Alberta. I *love* it. I'm not sure why. Sweeping up Albina and doing the streets off Albina, that's really fun. People say, 'Well, nobody even notices that you do it.' But it's like having clean sheets: you may not know they're clean but you're glad they're there."

Terry also sweeps Killingsworth which, like Albina, is a major arterial through the African-American community. "I think it's dirty because there's so much foot traffic in and out of the area. My need for gratification's really simple: it's a really dirty area and I can make it look good. The people who really live and work around there, they appreciate it. So that's kind of my idea of fun."

Terry doesn't have an exact number, but she figures her route covers between 250 and 350 miles. "In the summer, when it's a little bit lighter and I don't have the heavy leaves and I don't have gravel from snow and ice, I probably get through my route in three weeks. Something like that. Day shift, they have a lot more area to cover and I don't think they get through their maps nearly as quickly."

After her lunch break tonight, she plans to help out downtown, and so she crosses the river at 1:25 and parks the sweeper at NW 3rd and Flanders. A buncher picks her up there, and drives her across town to a well-known southeast Portland diner for lunch.

Sitting around a big table in Holman's, telling jokes with half a dozen burly bunchers and laborers, it's easy to see that Terry's gender and delicate size are not the only ways she's different from the crew.

Twenty-five years ago, she graduated with a BA in English and a teaching certificate in secondary education. She taught for a couple of years and then went to work in the Publications Department at Marylhurst College, where she stayed five years. "When I left Marylhurst I just couldn't stand it anymore. It was like too polite. I just wanted something really different."

She worked at a Christmas tree plantation for four years, shearing, fertilizing, and spraying, then left to get her masters in teaching at Portland State. "Originally I thought I wanted to have my own Christmas trees and if I taught, that would give me the summers to work on them."

In the summer she got work with the Parks Bureau because she'd had the Christmas tree background. "On the weekends I'd be a park attendant and we'd clean toilets and all that and that's how I got my foot in the door to get with the City." She never went back to teaching.

At 2:37 in the morning, lunch is over and Terry is back downtown. She turns on the sweeper and heads south on 3rd Avenue, dropping the broom just south of Burnside, where she begins to sweep the Rat Race.

Half a dozen teenagers are gathered on the curb in front of the Star Theater, and four more are across 3rd Avenue. At a red light, Terry studies eight people in front of Red Sea—dressed-up couples, two quartets. Even though the bars have just closed, there are still plenty of parked cars. At Jefferson, she turns west, where it's all been flushed, then north on 4th Avenue.

Remarkably, she can sweep between two parked cars. Her technique is to parallel park between them, then sharply angle in and out. It requires tension, alertness, precision. She picks up cans, paper cups, wrappers, and cigarettes, swiveling in and out from the curb.

Shortly after three, she's at the west end of the Hawthorne Bridge, where she turns and heads back west on Madison. And now, sweeping the left side of the street, just ahead of her, there's a Tymco, which is the other type of sweeper the City owns. It operates as a vacuum rather than with brooms and belt like the Elgin.

"About 4:00, 4:30 it really starts to pick up. Like if they're cleaning the Ross Island Bridge, they have to do a lot of traffic control, cause it's like somebody's opened a door.

"I usually start heading back about quarter to five. One of those things that the lucky laborers get to do is they get to wash the sweepers. They have a place called the hog pond, and two sweepers will fit in there with a catwalk in between. You'll have usually three laborers down there washing the different sweepers. While they're cleaning the outside, in theory, we're cleaning out the inside, getting the dust out and emptying any of our debris that we left.

"They don't like us to come up until 5:30. We fill out a couple of sheets; one is the status of the equipment, and then our time card. Then we sit around and bond for twenty minutes and read the paper. Sometimes people are real tired, sometimes they're real wired, you know. Sometimes people think, Oh I've just been driving, I can't read, I can't read anything tonight. We leave at six.

"I try to be in bed by seven. I have a black sheet over one window, and then I have a dark curtain over the other one. Somebody got me like a little eye patch—that helps a lot."

Working Monday through Friday, Terry's days off are Saturday and Sunday. She's single and enjoys gardening and walking. "There's a class you can take, it kind of helps you train to walk the marathon," she says, "so I do that." She also takes a class in *ashtanga* yoga, and has been going to the same book club for seventeen years. "The club was started with the idea that most people had professional jobs and that they didn't really feel that they had the time to read contemporary fiction," Terry says, although the list has strayed across genre lines. They just finished Thomas Friedman's *From Beirut to Jerusalem*, and next on the list is Bernard Malamud's *Magic Barrel*. The nine or ten club members have become so close that they always spend Thanksgiving together.

Terry's planning to stay on night shift, where she's fascinated by what she sees. "There are a lot more people out on the streets at night than I ever realized," she says. "I mean it's really busy but it never seems scary to me. I don't ever feel fearful.

"Usually everybody kind of nods. The guys that are out there, dealing drugs, everybody kind of nods. You know you got that kind of working wave that you do. If they're women who happen to be working, usually they kind of nod at you 'cause you're in a City rig and people assume that you're going to be pretty nice. [The prostitutes] may not realize I'm a woman, so they may wink or wave.

"And a garbage truck, if you're sweeping downtown you're always kind of jockeying around them. I just think it's a lot easier to wave to them rather than get grumpy. Once in a while you see drunk college kids goofing off, people horsing around.

"I've seen deer out on St. Helens Road. That was when I was bunching. I see raccoons, little things like that. Sometimes it's just incredibly beautiful, you know, like I've swept downtown and then we finish at quarter to five and come back and the sky will suddenly turn red. Or the fog will just descend and then as you start up the hill, it's like this blanket of fog and you see the tops of the buildings. Or the quality of the light at particular times of the year.

"I think it's very fun in the fall when the leaves come, and to just see the big blanket of yellow. I was just thinking about this the other night. There's been times when I've swept around Columbia Park and it's really quiet and all bright yellow, like a different kind of snow. You can't get very far 'cause you fill up very fast, but it's just way beautiful."

Up All Night

From Press to Porch

From SE Stark Street, it doesn't look like much: a nondescript office stuck in a long low building with no sign on the door. But at 12:30 in the morning, when the trucks arrive from downtown with the daily paper, the big room in the rear of this office is a lively hub of activity. Ten people are hurrying around stuffing advertising inserts and pre-run sections into the fresh papers, which then get folded and bagged and loaded into blue plastic shopping carts for transport to the parking lot out back, where the carriers' cars are waiting. In the midst of this bustle, serving coffee, making jokes, praising and thanking his staff or asking about their families is Tom Dietz. It's his office, his distributorship, and, in many ways, these are his people.

Trim and vigorous at sixty-four, Tom—as he prefers his crew to call him— has been with the *Oregonian* for forty-two years. As a distributor, he is a self-employed contractor. Tom estimates there to be 124 distributors in the Portland area. "We distribute to the households," he explains. "We don't sell on the street corners. We're expected to promote the area, find new customers to replace the ones that fall off."

Tom began in 1957, seven years after the paper, then in its 106th year of local ownership, was sold to the Newhouse Newspaper Group. In those days, the company put out two papers a day. "Normally anybody just getting started got an evening *Oregonian* area first," Tom recalls. "Then you kind of got moved into the morning-only one, and then eventually you got a morning and evening combined."

In four decades of selling the paper, Tom has seen a lot of changes. "Those were the days, when we had kids delivering," he says, recalling when last he used bicycle delivery. "We can't possibly use kids today. Papers are too humongous, and there's no way they could carry them. Even the adults with their routes, which of course are bigger than kids' routes were, they have to make two or three trips on Sundays."

Tom is responsible for overseeing the delivery of about eighteen hundred daily papers, and close to two thousand on Sunday to the two neighborhoods with zip code 97216, Montavilla and Russellville. For this work, he hires an assistant and contracts eight carriers and several other people who sort and stack newsprint. The first five carriers meet the 12:30 truck.

"You open up when the paper arrives. The company does not own any rolling stock so they use contract haulers to bring the papers out to us."

Along with the paper, the carriers get an equal amount of pre-runs, that is, weekly sections that are printed and delivered ahead of time, such as Tuesday's *FOODday*, Thursday's *Home & Garden*, Friday's *A&E*, along with advertisers' inserts, which require very particular placement between designated sections. "Those can create headaches and problems," Tom says. "Of course it doesn't end with that. Last Saturday morning, we had a special bag with a sample product in it, barbecue sauce."

This collating is done by hand and often takes longer than the actual delivery. The back room in which Tom's crew does this work is big and bright, with seven separate working surfaces. The last step is to put the paper in a plastic bag.

"The company runs like five editions," Tom explains, "and the I-205 freeway splits my area. I get one truck for the customers east of the freeway, and that comes in around 12:30, the mid-county edition. Then the Portland edition, which is this side of the freeway, comes in to us about 2:30. Three carriers is all I have on the Portland edition, right now." Those three arrive to meet the second truck.

Technically, Tom no longer has to come down here personally because he has an assistant, Dan, whose responsibility it is to open in the morning and make sure everything is carried out. "Even if I'm here, he's still supposed to do his thing," Tom explains. But Tom is often here. "You just kind of go in for the moral support. I mean, they have to do the hard work so I figure that they should see me in there." On Sunday mornings, when the papers are heavier and there are more of them, Tom brings his carriers doughnuts and Pepsi.

It's hard to get and keep good people because the work is seven days a week and the monthly pay is not great. Dan has been with Tom for four years, which is considered a long time in this business. Right now, the senior carrier has been with Tom for three years. A father-daughter team used to have a route and now come in during the day to do the pre-stacking of inserts and pre-runs. "If you counted that, they've been with me probably about eight years," Tom points out.

Carriers are paid per newspaper. For two hours delivery time, and then whatever it takes to get the paper ready to go out in the morning, most carriers average around $650 per month.

"You never know until they've been with you probably a month," Tom says. "You can't even tell after a week or so. It grinds on them after a while if they've got a wife and family at home, and they're getting up in the middle of the night. The ideal situation is if you can find somebody that has a job where they get off about one in the morning or somebody that goes to work around seven in the morning.

"The fellow who's still with me three years or so, he's retired from the Highway Department, so he gets a pretty good pension from them. He's not real old. He makes about eight to nine hundred a month on his route."

One carrier is a stay-at-home dad who plays in a band on weekends. "We call and wake him up every morning," Tom says, indulgently. "We're his alarm clock."

Because Dan helps with the inserting, the papers on the second truck get out pretty fast. "And I have one woman that works once her husband gets out. He's on the early truck. Then she hangs around with Dan and she helps the people on the second truck get out. On a problem-free morning, the second group of carriers spend no more than about two and a half hours a morning, total."

Many mornings are not problem-free. "The truck comes late usually once or twice a week. It's the presses. Mechanical problems are the big problem. If I didn't have them by quarter to two, I would probably call. If they tell you the truck left at one, you figure, well, boy, something happened! It doesn't take forty-five minutes to get here." The truck comes from the production plant on SW Taylor Street downtown.

When the truck is late, the carriers don't get extra money for waiting around, but they do get extra stress because the deadline for getting the paper to the customer is still 5:30 a.m.

Tom is grateful for the goodwill with which the carriers handle these emergencies. He has decorated the office walls with birthday banners and notes of appreciation and framed photographs of his distributorship picnics. "We strive to do the best," says Tom, whose distributorship has frequently been cited by the *Oregonian* for sales and retention. "My help takes pride because we usually are the top bunch. It's a good feeling."

On a good night, the last carrier would go out the door about 3:30. "From that point the main role is to get the paper up to the customer, and the main purpose is the customer's satisfaction."

A carrier's success depends, to some extent, on how Tom has engineered the route. "Some routes are just porch delivery, where the carrier has to get out of the car almost at every stop. I try to keep most of my routes, the porch delivery routes, at 200, 225 daily papers.

"Some of it you can stuff out the car window. Out in suburbia, we use paper tubes." Unless they're right along the roadway, however, tubes elsewhere usually end up being a nuisance. "We try to discourage porch tubes 'cause they're more trouble for the carrier. If you have a good carrier on the route, and he can slide the paper up by the door, there isn't any need for him to walk up another twenty steps."

When the carriers leave, Tom does not go home to bed. "You don't want to just see the last guy out the door and then forget it," he points out, "because a lot of the people you're dealing with don't have brand new cars, of course, and a lot of times you're out there jump-starting an automobile."

Carrier Anita Smith, thirty-six, drives a 1994 Ford Taurus four-door station wagon. "This has been the most dependable vehicle I've owned," she says. "I bought it last year for $8,400. The last one was a 1987 Dodge Aries which I had for a year, and that car broke down at every turn." Anita still carries a cell phone, just as protection.

Her route is a mixture of tubes and porches, and includes stretches of cul-de-sacs with no sidewalks, the kind of neighborhood that discourages any mode of travel except the automobile. This can be a problem when there are four vehicles in the driveway and no front walk from the sidewalk to the porch. The only access to the porch is that paved driveway, and every vehicle has a car alarm.

"And they don't want you walking on the lawn," Anita says. "They can see your tracks and where you've been and they call up and say, 'The carrier's been on the lawn.'"

Since she and her husband separated, Anita's ten-year-old son, Jeremy, sleeps a split shift and comes with her on her route, because she feels she cannot leave him at home in the care of his twelve-year-old brother. "Jeremy helps me deliver my porches," she says. "We'll do 124 in thirty minutes." Alone, the same number of papers takes her forty-five minutes. On Sundays, her route shoots up to 350 subscribers, but then she's got both boys with her.

Anita is thankful to Tom, who not only tolerates the addition of her kids but takes an interest in them and their schoolwork. "There needs to be more men around like him. He's the type that will give everybody a last chance, and then another one, too."

Tom Dietz was born and raised in southeast Portland. "I've lived here all my life. I went to Our Lady of Sorrows grade school, to Central Catholic for one year, and three years to Franklin High.

"I worked as an assistant to the old circulation manager, Pat Marlton, when he was a dealer, and then I went in the Navy for two years." Tom was married in 1955 when he got out of the Navy.

"I drove a city bus for a year and a half. I had a good reputation there, but it wasn't something I wanted to do all my life. I kind of liked the newspaper business, so I went back to try to get into it." That's when he got his first dealership (the *Oregonian* has since switched over to distributorships). It was here in Montavilla, although he would move to Rose City after only nine months.

Tom's wife has always stayed at home. "And I pat her on the back," he says, "because when we were running both the *Oregonian* morning and evening, I was hardly ever home. So I commend her for putting up with that and for doing such a great job of raising our two kids." Now those kids are forty and Tom is happily involved with his grandchildren.

"I've kind of enjoyed the sense of freedom that I've had. I'm not punching a time clock. My wife and I do not go too many places out of town; it's not like we have a cabin up in the mountains or out at the beach and take off every weekend, so usually I'm here. Even if I don't get up early in the mornings on the weekends, I still stay in contact.

"You don't have the company benefits, that's one of the bad things; you have to make your own benefits. But I chose to do it this way, and I've never been sorry. I could have gone in and been a company employee and had weekends off and all that kind of good stuff. But I've just kind of enjoyed what I've done."

In the Stark Street office at 3:30 in the morning, it's too early to return phone calls, but Tom can work on billings, organize new route lists, read the mail, or respond to cries for help from his carriers. He has a keen imagination for the problems of new carriers just starting out. "It's dark out there, they're fighting a list and a flashlight and probably rain and everything else. Dogs barking. At least this leash law has done a great job of keeping them in, but usually they're barking."

After all these years, Tom is still puzzled by some of the mail he gets. "You get the kind where they call the carrier an idiot, or 'Why can't he get it on the porch? I delivered papers when I was a kid. I know what it's all about.'

"Well, they don't know what it's all about. All they need to do is get up and come in for a couple of days and they can see it's not like it was when they were a little kid.

"And then you get the snide remarks when they send their payments: 'I would have sent this in sooner if the paper would have been closer to the door.'

"They don't realize how many people we go through. Sometimes, within a year's time, we'll go through five or six people on one route, if it's not that great a route. And every time you put a new person on, you'll get another call from the people: 'Why can't that carrier do that? He was doing okay.' 'Well, sir, it's a new carrier.' 'Well, can't you keep carriers?'"

But there are also notes that say, simply: 'Please thank the carrier.' And Tom does.

In bad weather, he sits by the phone. "I'd have to say ice is the worst. People don't understand it. You're running real late on those days and you'll get a call from some customer who only takes the Sunday: 'I'd sure like to have a daily today if you could possibly get the carrier to leave me one.' Because she's sure she's not going to be able to get out of the house. Or else you get the other people who just look out their door and don't realize what the streets are like and then they can't understand why you can't get to them.

"It seems on a bad night Murphy's Law takes over, and there's more than just one problem. You have a lot of thick papers *and* inserts *and* a product. You walk in and pick up your recorder and somebody says they're not going to be in. Well, you live with that. You wish they'd let you know the night before, so that could build your mind to it, but you tell Dan what's happening. Next somebody's car breaks down, so you might have to come out and help them or drive them around. People get flat tires.

"But the area isn't that big, and there's a pay phone almost on every corner, so they either call or make it back to the station somehow. Dan has a cell phone, and of course I have one. We try to stay in touch and anticipate problems. If somebody leaves here and we've had to jump their battery before they can even leave, then we go out and check on them to make sure they're moving."

As the morning wears on, he'll begin to get the missed-paper calls. While he's always polite to the customer, he understands how something like that can happen. "It's all memory type work, there's two hundred customers, so you could forget to cross the street or something, or somebody could steal it." These days, Dan is generally the one to run missed papers to customers.

"And we get a lot of calls that aren't true calls. Some woman will call and demand her paper, and when you get there, she apologizes 'cause her husband brought it in and didn't tell her.

"We've had carriers that have gotten out of their cars and delivered a paper and come back and the car's gone! With all the papers. The first thing you do is call the police, of course, about the car. And then you start making phone calls to the sales representative and let him know that you need a hundred fifty extra papers, and he'll get on the phone and try to find out where some might be. You call around. There's a lot of us will have ten or twenty left over in the morning sometimes, like samples we didn't use or something, so you try to scrounge anything you can.

"A good night, you open up, and everybody would show up on time, and the papers are on time, and everybody gets out of here."

On such a night, Tom sits in tranquility, alone at his desk, in the nondescript office on Stark Street, below framed plaques of appreciation from his staff.

"And then I might not really have anything I'm doing. It's still too early to make customer contacts, so I'll have a cup of coffee and just read the paper."

Up All Night

Tech Support

Curt Deardorff is a twenty-five-year-old boy genius who works nights in an industrial area near the east end of the Ross Island bridge. His large second story office is honeycombed with one hundred cubicles, all of them covered in grey-green carpet—one hundred little padded cells. Curt's cube, like all the others, has an L-shaped desk with a computer and a phone, and a chair on which he can roll around his cube. Tonight, his black hooded sweatshirt hangs over the door.

At 11:00 p.m., Curt is on the phone with a woman from Pennsylvania. He's already gotten her name, phone number, and login or user name. "I'm looking for your account right now," he tells her. He wears a headset, which leaves his hands free to work the keyboard.

"Excuse me," she says. "I'm so dumb at this."

"No, you're doing okay," he says. He's found her account now and asks whether she's on Windows 95 or 98.

"Windows 98, I'm pretty sure," she says.

"How can I help you now?"

"I cannot send or receive email," she says.

"Okay, did you get an error message?" Curt asks.

She's not sure.

"That's okay," he says. "How do you know you don't have email?"

"People send me email but I don't receive it," she explains.

"What is the name of your email program?"

"Netscape?"

"Go ahead and bring it up," he tells her.

"Will I be able to get on email while I'm talking to you?" she asks.

"Do you just have one phone line?"

"Yes."

"Then, no—but that's okay. Bring up Netscape."

And as she's doing that, Curt has one of the small intuitive flashes which punctuate his evening: "When Alltel took Apollo over," he asks her, "did you make arrangements through customer service for Alltel to start hosting your account?"

116

After a pause, she says, "I didn't know I needed to do that."

He encourages her to take care of it in the morning, and the phone call is over. He wishes out loud that people would remember to write down their error messages. "Like one line, *user unknown,* can be fixed by just going in and looking at the syntax of their email address."

As the lead technician on graveyard, Curt helps people get and stay connected to the Internet. He's employed by 800-Support, whose business it is to "outsource" or lend their technical support to Internet service providers from all over the United States. In Curt's case, he provides tech support for Alltel, a huge telephone company "back East." As a member of the Alltel team, Curt takes calls from customers in Arkansas, North Carolina, and Pennsylvania.

"Where you are and what you look like doesn't really matter," Curt says. "The main thing with this company is customer service and getting the calls answered." Tonight, Curt wears a blue and green batik t-shirt and blue jeans. He's got brown eyes, chin-length hair, and two days' beard growth. He's twitchy, energetic, and boyishly cute.

"It's like an unspoken law that you do the best you can to help the customer," Curt says. "But you have to have a decision point where, if this call has gone too long, yes, maybe I could help them but, yes, maybe it's going to take another half an hour. So you do what you need to do to get rid of them legitimately. A lot of the time I can easily get rid of somebody, because even though I've maybe spent twenty minutes helping them, once I'm done I'm still going to send them to their manufacturer to get the right driver for their modem. You use that kind of an excuse to get off the phone."

The longest call Curt can remember was two hours and fifteen minutes.

"Usually the company wants you to keep your calls ideally to ten minutes. If it goes to half an hour, either you can't fix their problem or you're not taking charge of the call and getting their butt in gear. It's a real art. I mean you can't rush people, but they kind of want you to rush them. You can't piss people off, but you've got to. Sometimes you've got to shut people up and just get them to focus. You know, just step-by-step, let's do this and get it over with, I don't have time to chat with you."

Since most of his customers are on the East Coast and there's a three-hour time difference, the most active hours on his shift are from ten to eleven at night, when he first comes on. It slows down and then picks up again around 4:00 a.m. and stays busy until Curt gets off work at seven. The pattern varies at other 800-Support offices (Alltel maintains three in Oregon), where other ISP clients may be on local time. The number of people working any given shift depends on which ISPs the 800-Support office is serving, and where their customers are. Tonight there are twenty-two people here in the SE Gideon office; on day shift there may be anywhere from thirty to sixty, with forty or fifty on swing.

"When I get here I usually check with the [swing shift] lead. If nothing is down, then we just start taking calls as usual. But if a location is down, you know, everybody and their brother is calling in. They're calling from Richmond, Virginia, and I can say, 'No sense in even trying to solve this problem right now. We're down in that area, so I'll see you later, guy. Sorry.'

"I'm technically the person in charge. If something goes wrong, I have to fix it. I don't get paid much more money for it; it's just sort of a position. I trained every single person who's ever been moved up, and I'm sort of left behind because I choose to stay on the graveyard shift. A lot of times [being lead tech] probably just isn't worth the trouble. I really only stay at that job because right now the graveyard shift works out for me.

"As in most tech support centers, we have lower-quality, older machines at our cubicles than what the customers will be calling us about. Ours are okay: most of them are either Pentium 166 or 200s, which are nice and fast and everything, but by today's standards are kind of old and dumpy. Most of the computers have 32 megs of RAM, so that's nice. Most of us have speakers, sound cards—they make it enjoyable for us. Between calls we can surf the Net, listen to some CDs or whatever.

"For such a prestigious company, I would definitely get computer systems that are up-to-date, but at the same time I understand that they're doing the best they can. It's one thing to buy a few brand new computers for your few employees; it's another thing to buy a whole building full of them. But from what I hear, interoffice rumors and stuff, the owner of the company is not hurting. The guy drives a very expensive car.

"So, yeah, I think improvements could be done on the equipment. I think we could have better equipment. But overall, over other jobs I've had, I think this is probably the best equipment I've had for Internet tech support."

Entirely self-taught, Curt is now working his third tech support job. Eight years ago, in San Luis Obispo, he was a high school dropout.

"I left high school because I wasn't getting good grades—Ds and Fs. I was going to go to community college and kind of finish up that way. It was great. You went there for like half a day, high school without all the BS, and it worked great for me. Still didn't graduate. Toward the end there, I was still a few credits short. Ninety-two should have been my graduation year.

"I took the GED when I moved to Utah. Surprised at how easy it was to pass. Then I took the occasional college course here and there just for the heck of it. But being sort of a Generation Xer, I honestly feel my generation gave up the whole you-have-to-do-college-right-out-of-high-school idea years ago. It's ridiculous.

"I'd say I got into computers more when Windows 95 came out. My dad had an old Windows 3.1, 386 computer, mostly DOS, but I wasn't really into computers back then."

In Salt Lake, one of Curt's friends bought a computer and told him, "I can get you a job working at this cool place. If you know a little bit about Windows, we can get you trained and on the phones." That's how Curt started working at Sisna. "Little did I know how little I knew," he says today.

"They didn't train me. They threw me on the phones and I would blow out every single call. It was a small Ma-and-Pa place. If it had been any other place, I probably would have been fired, but they gave me a chance. Constantly asking questions, constantly trying to get what the heck I was doing."

Curt worked two and a half years for Sisna in Salt Lake City before moving to Portland. "It's really taken years," he says now, "but I just kind of learned it."

He worked for Stream International in Beaverton for a year and then came over to 800-Support in the winter of 1997-98. Now, after six years in the business, he knows exactly what he's doing.

"I don't mean to boast, but hey, what the heck. Very rarely do I have a problem where I really can't fix it. It's only going to go two ways: either you're going to hang up with the problem fixed, or you're going to hang up and do something that I told you to do, try it out, follow it through. Hardly any of my problems are unsolved because I can almost always pin them on something. And if I don't know what the problem is, I still have a pretty good hunch."

Three problems show up again and again, night after night.

"There's like a whole series of errors that you can get using a program called Dialup Networking, and they're just general errors. They all sound a little bit different but they're all commonly referred to as general dialogue networking errors. They're usually caused by wrong user name, wrong password—in other words, user error, about 90 percent of the time. Then there's a small percentage of the time that it's their settings. No matter what the customer thinks when they call, 99.9 percent of the time it's the customer.

"The second most common call would be like email problems, 'I can't get my email.' It's usually related to the first problem. They haven't realized that while they're sitting there trying to get email, they're not connected. Period. Or they have wrong email settings. 'Cause with email programs, if you're one single setting off, you're screwed.

"And then the third most common would be 'I can connect, but I cannot browse.' It shows that they're connected on their operating systems, but when they go to actually trying to use the browser and go to different sites, none of the sites will work. That's usually due to a settings problem."

On the wall, a sign reads: *Sir, WHAT was the last thing that happened before your system got hosed?*

Curt's talent consists not only in diagnosing, but in describing the problem and the remedy in low-tech terms, a language he's mastered.

"The network's criss-crossed like a spiderweb. We already had a mess of phone lines here in the U.S. We already had all that set up in the early eighties, seventies, around there, whatever. The Internet started with the military, moved to where they'd connect universities, and then they said, 'Gee, let's start the Internet. Let's start a worldwide web, why not?' And the Internet's grown from there on.

"So you dial from your house into the Internet. The signal leaves your house—it's really random, you have no control over it—and it may go through and make a left instead of a right, or whatever. It goes through *this* telephone line, *that* telephone line, maybe through a crappy part of town where there are old telephone lines. Or maybe you're lucky and it goes through all brand new telephone lines.

"But it goes like this," he scrambles his fingers the way that toddlers find delightfully scary. "All the way through it hits different routers here and there, maybe this router's up, maybe this one's down. It's amazing it works. To get from point A to point B on the Internet, if it can't send it this way it will send it this way. If it can't send it this way it will send it *this* way. Whatever it has to do in the web, it gets the signal from point A to B. That's how the Internet works. It's pretty amazing."

Curt is sympathetic with his customers who hate computers. "They're horribly slow!" he says. "I think computers actually are just now starting to catch up to people's attention spans. We're on the tip of the iceberg right now. We have to let *userability*—that's a term—catch up with technology before people will really start to enjoy computers. Same thing here. I've only really enjoyed computers this last couple of years."

Now that he's enjoying them, he's finally begun to take some classes. At Pioneer Pacific College, he's enrolled in a program which will earn him an Associate of Applied Science degree in fifteen months. "Right now I'm going for network administrator. It's what everybody is going for right now. It's booming because everybody's setting up a network of computers in their office, and everybody's connecting the networks together in that building, and everybody's hooking all that network up to the Internet. It's happening everywhere, in every building, everywhere. That's why network admins are in demand. So that's what I'm going for. Do I want to? No. I'd really rather live out in the woods and be nature boy. But, it's what you got to do. You got to play the game for a while."

At night, after the East Coast rush has slowed down, Curt does his homework. "Depending on the classes I'm taking. Some of them I can genuinely learn without doing a whole lot of studying, just by paying attention closely when I'm there. But if I need to study, I get most of that done at work. There's no other time I have to do it."

Curt's schedule is tight. "I get off at 7:00, school begins at 7:50, and then I usually have classes anywhere from that time till like, if I'm lucky, 11:30. But some mods, which is the equivalent to like a semester, I have a class that's going all the way til 1:40, and then I don't get home til 2:00. Then I go to sleep immediately, wake up around 8:00, have about an hour to spend with Emily and our little boy, Oscar."

Oscar, who's three, is the reason Curt works nights and Emily works days. "We make sure that he has to have daycare the least amount of time as possible."

On graveyard, Curt generally takes lunch around 1:00 a.m., and he often spends the hour sleeping outside in his car. "Or I'll drive around a bit, I'll go to Taco Bell or whatever."

By two o'clock in the morning, when he gets back, there are two more hours to get through before the calls begin to pick up.

"Typical guy, I play games. There's a whole series of games nowadays that instead of just shoot 'em up bang-bang, it's like looking at a map. The games that me and my friends like to play are like Starcraft, where you kind of build *this* to get *that*." Hanging on the wall of his cube is a colorful Starcraft poster, which claims to be the **Best Strategy Game Yet**.

"We play network games. A real popular one is Quake and you can play it over the Internet. They don't let you do it during the day cause it takes up bandwidth, which is what they pay a lot of money for. It slows everyone else down—obviously not job related. But at night, there's only a few of us there, so who cares if we're taking up a lot of bandwidth? It's not going to affect anybody. What you do is, I'm sitting at my computer, he's sitting at his; I'm this person running around shooting at him and he's doing the same. So that can be really fun to pass the time.

"To be honest, I do a lot of surfing on the Internet. You can never say that you've looked up everything on the Internet. It's endless. You have to limit yourself. You can get into different university databases, and just pick a subject. One of my favorite hobbies is reading everything I can about Egyptology.

"If I'd had unlimited resources and funds and could have gone to university like a rich kid and gone for something that's impractical, I always wanted to be an archaeologist. I would be happy getting out of this damn cube and spending the rest of my life in the dirt, in a ditch somewhere digging up two-thousand-year-old bones."

At three in the morning, one of Curt's coworkers is lying on the carpeted floor of his cube, talking into his headset. "I'm actually in Portland, Oregon," he's saying. "Yeah, you got to open up Internet Explorer to do that." "Well, if you get any more problems just call me back and we'll go from there." "My name's Dennis. Thanks for calling Alltel Support."

"Who cares if you're sitting in a chair or lying down?" Curt remarks. "I mean, come on. It's late at night, there's not a call for an hour. If you've got your headset on your head you can jump up and grab on your computer, do whatever you want." In fact, as Curt knows, many of these guys can walk a customer through a call without even looking at their own computer.

"I'm sure if you went to my boss right now, he'd say, 'No, that never happens.' But when he's not around, sure it happens all the time.

"A night person, a true night person who isn't just working the graveyard shift temporarily a couple of months out of the year [but] who really likes it, is usually a weird, quirky person," Curt says. "Usually, you know, Bohemian or maybe even a social misfit. I notice a lot of night-time people are really weird. Like not cool-weird: I'm talking about weird like in the head, like they have social skill problems. Day people tend to be more peppy and more buying into the whole rat race. I don't know how to describe it."

Curt takes a call. "Do you have your user name and password and everything?" he asks.

"How old is it?" he asks.

"Is it like Windows 95 or Windows 98?" he asks.

"How can I help you?

"I see. And did it give you an error message?"

Outside his cube, a posted slogan reads: **Alltel—the power to simplify begins with me**.

Up All Night

All-Night Poolroom

"Pool is a lifestyle for me. It's my recreation, my love, my work," says Jim Mosher, a twenty-two-year-old pool player who works nights at Cue's Billiards in southeast Portland. "I have dreams about it. I wake in the middle of the night with my bridge hand *like this*, like I'm holding a pool cue. I'll be in a dream and I'll see a three-wheel shot, a nine-ball stroke shot that I'd like to do one day."

The billiard parlors of northwest Portland take American Express and sell single-malt scotches with more years on them than Jim Mosher himself, but the eastside poolrooms are something else. There's a line from *The Hustler*, where Fast Eddie Felson first arrives at Ames, hoping to meet up with Minnesota Fats. "No bar?" Eddie asks, figuring he's in for a wait. And the owner assures him, "No bar, no pinball machines, no bowling alleys, just pool. Nothing else. This is Ames, Mister." The same might be said of Cue's. It's all business.

Cue's is vast, nearly ten thousand square feet of floor space covered with one of the most lavish carpets in town—golden circlets of wheat are repeated every thirty inches over a rich field of burgundy. When Caesars Palace was remodeled a few years back, Ron Springman, who owns Cue's, bought the carpet second-hand, and it lends a garish glamor to an otherwise nondescript room of pale green walls and a few inconspicuous wooden support posts. Propeller fans spin listlessly overhead, although no smoking is allowed. Spread across the burgundy wool carpet are thirty-seven pool tables, each covered in rich green felt, and above each of them hangs an inverted gray oblong box of diffused electronic ballast lights. Professional grade, the lights don't even flicker. It's a clean facility—vacuumed, neat, orderly—and the only poolroom in Portland that stays open twenty-four hours.

"Cue's before was an unemployment office," Jim Mosher says. "And Cue's *now*, if you look at the people that hang out there during the daylight hours, it's still an unemployment office. They don't have jobs, they have nowhere else to go."

Jim works an erratic on-call graveyard shift which may mean 1:00 a.m. to eight, or 3:00 a.m. to eleven, whatever's needed during the hours that are typically slowest at Cue's. He's stationed at an elevated counter in one elbow of the T-shaped room, from where he can survey everything. Customers may be playing snooker, for which Cue's has three special twelve-foot tables; billiards, for which Cue's has four tables without pockets; or, more commonly, one of half a dozen different games of pool, the most common being eight-ball and nine-ball.

It's Jim's duty to distribute the racks of balls and then calculate how much the players owe when they turn them back in. "They can't just say, 'Here's five dollars, give me a rack of balls,'" Jim explains. "It's based on how much time they played, how many people they had with them, what table they played on, and what hour of the day. It's a bunch of if-and-then statements, like in electronics.

"For premium tables you're going to pay four dollars an hour for one person, seven dollars an hour for two, eight-fifty an hour for three, and ten dollars an hour for four. Now that's premium prices between 5:00 p.m. and 8:00 a.m. And then on the other side, with the normal tables, we have four dollars an hour, five dollars an hour, six dollars an hour, and seven dollars an hour, something like that. But then it's much less expensive during the day. Now on holidays, it's premium prices all the time, unless, of course, it's daytime. And then if you have people jumping on and off the table, they don't want to pay for four people all the time. Let's say this third person is like, 'I want to play. No, I guess I don't want to play. Okay, well, I want to play.' I have to keep track of that for every single table."

Besides calculating the tab, Jim rents pool cues for a dollar to those who want something a little better than right off the rack and, from the other end of the counter ("Cue's Corner Pocket Restaurant"), he sells hamburgers, pizza, corn dogs, burritos, coffee, and soft drinks.

Five foot five, blonde hair prematurely receding, wearing baggy pants, Jim has an open smile and a friendly manner. Many people recognize him. "I can't go three minutes without having somebody say, 'Hey, Jim, what's up?' 'Hey, Jim, how you doing?'" To an already long list of things Jim loves about pool, he would add the social element. "It's indoors, it's warm, it's heated, and it's something that people can do together. It's a relaxing thing, you can sit back and talk to people at the same time."

His gregarious personality helps him keep Cue's the safe, drug-free place the owner expects it to be. Jim is proud of Cue's, advertised as "The largest billiard room on the West Coast," and he's also seen what can happen in other pool halls when the discipline is lax.

"I can think of many a friend that's been stabbed because of *that* place," Jim says, naming an all-night bowling alley which has eleven pool tables in front. "There's a bar right there, [an adult] dance place down the street. Bingo! You're asking for trouble there, and getting it. I've been down there numerous times when people have got pool cues busted over their heads.

"There's been trouble at Cue's, too," Jim explains. "But 90 percent of it we've kicked out. I'd say once a month we might have a fight where people start yelling and pushing each other, and I'd say once every six months to a year we have a fight where people actually throw punches. But that's all swing shift stuff, between like 6:00 p.m. and 2:00 a.m.

"And, once again, associated with any twenty-four-hour place, you're going to have drugs. That's a given. You're going to have marijuana, crank, coke, heroin, acid—I mean you're going to *see* it in there. And when we do, we throw it out."

Springman, the lanky, pale-skinned owner, has a grudge against drugs, and thinks nothing of calling Narcotics if he suspects someone is dealing in his poolroom. A Vietnam vet, he saw Army buddies wasted on heroin. A former pool champion, he's seen excellent players blow out on amphetamines or coke.

Jim is also expected to discourage hustling. "Generally speaking," Jim says, "hustling doesn't happen like people make it sound—like you're just pretending you play extremely bad, and you're slowly getting better and better, and pretty soon you have ten thousand dollars in your pocket. It's not like that.

"Generally speaking, when people go on the road they're usually going on their way to a tournament, just like in *The Color of Money*. And they don't go there pretending to be nobody, they go there saying, 'I'm looking for money.' They might not play their complete capacity, they might play just well enough to beat the other player."

That "just well enough" is what Springman doesn't want at Cue's. Since opening the poolroom in 1995, he's discouraged the action players, because he doesn't want them hustling the regular customers who are his bread and butter. "It takes me five minutes to spot a hustler," says Springman, who was once an action player as well as a tournament champion ."I can watch a guy play and see right away if he's laying down."

Tournaments are another matter. Cue's has a Thursday night nine-ball tournament for B and below, and is trying to establish a Tuesday night open tournament. "B and below," Jim explains, "means you can be a B player, you can be a C player; you just can't enter if you're an A.

"B players would be at a good solid skill level: they can shoot well, there's consistency to their game, they know the shots, whereas a C player might not be able to look at all the avenues. So that's how you classify them—a player's knowledge and ability to stroke a ball. C is novice, A is semi-pro."

When Jim is not on shift, likely as not he's at Cue's shooting pool. He figures he's shooting pool thirty-five, forty hours a week. "Some days I might play two hours, some days I might play ten." He favors nine-ball, which is the game Fast Eddie Felson has to get accustomed to in the 1986 film, *The Color of Money*. (In *The Hustler*, the same character shoots straight pool, which is a different game.) In the fourteen years since Scorsese's film came out, there has been a renaissance of pool in the United States, with many of the new pool halls affecting an upscale decor, with fresh flowers and a gentleman's club appeal. Not so at Cue's, where a sign hand-lettered in felt tip pen warns you to **Keep your Shirt on your Back and your Bike Outside**.

"When it comes to nine-ball, some people are luckier than others," Jim contends. "And it's really not luck, because your brain has learned it. Every shot, everything you do, is remembered in your head, and it's just how well you can bring those things out of the background of your mind into the foreground, where you're using your conscious skills to play on the table."

Though Jim only began playing in earnest about three years ago, he has been around pool ever since he was a child.

"My dad's a longshoreman and he used to hang out at a bar down near the waterfront. It's called Molly Maguire's—it's still down there. There's a little pool table in there, and that's the first table I ever remember shooting on. I was like six years old, five years old.

"I moved around a lot because my mom died when I was younger. I had my first apartment when I was thirteen. I was getting my mother's social security, so that would be six hundred dollars a month, and I moved in with a roommate who was nineteen or twenty years old. I was thirteen years old and paying half the rent.

"I would just go to school for a while and see where the parties were later on that night. Finally at the end of '97 I got my GED. At least I got that. But I mean it was hard because I didn't have anybody to say, 'Get up and go to school.' I didn't have anybody.

"I got exposed to all the drugs really early. I think I got drunk more times before my fifteenth birthday than I have in the last four years. There's still not a lot of things that I won't try, not many things that I will say absolutely *No* to.

"As far as who I am today—I would be totally different without all the drugs I did, without all the sex I had, and all the beer that I drank, and without my mom dying. I would be a completely different person."

From his elevated corner perch, Jim turns his attention to a game of one-pocket nearby. A player is poised for a bank shot which may—or may not—sink the yellow ball into his designated pocket. The player, a massive Polynesian man wearing a John Deere cap, makes his shot, and Jim raises an eyebrow appreciatively. One-pocket is fairly rare, at Cue's or anywhere.

"I still like to go out and party till like seven o'clock in the morning. I haven't seen daylight in maybe three days, four days. It's not that I'm choosing to be that, it's just the way I end up. I'm going to do things right now that people may still not like, but they don't affect other people. See I am a very nice person. There's not too many people I can say wouldn't like me, or don't like me. I can't think of *any* people that hate me. Maybe an ex-girlfriend or so, but other than that …

"I've taken a lot of trials through my life. Sometimes things are still tough, you know, but it's all part of getting older."

Jim counts five separate times he's been employed at Cue's. "Essentially, whenever they need somebody they call me. I've sold cars. I build my own computers. I buy parts, assemble them, put them together. I've messed around with them, just kind of picked and probed, picked different people's heads, asked them a lot of questions. But I've never opened a book. Never, ever. I do HTML programming, graphics, animation, stuff like that. I think if I *were* to open a book and read about computers and programming, I could be a lot better than I am.

"You give me a Rubik's Cube or something like that, and I'll play with it for days. Just keep it in my pocket until I get it right. I like to analyze things. I was taking apart VCRs when I was four years old.

"Pool is a game that is 90 percent mental. You're trying to map out three or four shots ahead so that way you know kind of a route you need to take. The greatest opponent in pool is the table. It doesn't matter *who* you're playing; you're playing the table: those balls are different every time. When you're in dead stroke, you're not thinking about anything but the table, and what's out there, and how you're going to get to that nine-ball, to knock it in. When I'm in dead stroke I'm not missing, I'm freewheeling, I'm hitting them in, they're going."

Jim sips from a large Coke. Except for the constant smack of balls and the occasional slam and clatter of a break shot, the poolhall is fairly quiet.

"I have many, many dreams and aspirations in pool. It teaches me a lot. Sometimes it teaches me to be patient; sometimes it teaches me to be aggressive, depending on the pace of my opponent. Because people play at certain speeds. Some people may take half a second a shot, some people might take thirty seconds. It depends what kind of game you're playing. Pool will teach you to either slow down and think, or that you should get up and go.

"I considered myself a pool player when I noticed that I had enough skill to do the things I wanted to do on the pool table, to put the ball where I wanted. That's when I was like, God, I've got to get good at this. And I have one goal—I want to be an A player by the end of this year."

On Jim's shift, business can be slow. If there were a dozen tables occupied at 11:00, there may be only two or three tables in use at 3:00 am. Usually, it will be a twosome shooting recreational pool, or perhaps a single dedicated pool player, practicing. Once in a while there may be an all-night session. On the rare occasions that two action players show up, a match may go all night. At Cue's, the longest session Jim has seen was thirty-three hours, though he wasn't there for the whole time. "It started at like 10:30 at night," he recalls.

Pool's nocturnal tradition is simple, according to Jim: "Daylight throws off the light on the tables. That's why, if you look at Cue's, it has no windows. If you go to like Jillian's up in Tacoma, there's windows everywhere and during the daytime you can't play shit just because there's so much light. It casts different shadows on the balls and your eyes perceive the balls differently."

Jim sees a little daylight on the way home—he's back living with his dad again, after ten years. When he wakes, it's dark again. Generally, he'll sleep a few hours, get up, eat, and double back to Cue's. "I mean we live right down the street. I'm either home or I'm at Cue's. That's about the only two places I go.

"Sometimes I'll just sit and do drills. I'll shoot certain shots all day and just try to find out what I'm doing wrong. Or I might just shoot balls and won't knock them into pockets. There'll be a day when I might be feeling bad: I'll just make simple shots all day, try and build my confidence back up. And then I'll start shooting better, and then I'll feel good about myself. And then I'll get off the table and just walk outside of the pool hall and go, Ahhh, God, I feel better. I mean, that's how much pool does for me.

"Right now, pool is the one thing I can count on in my life, the thing that I know will always be there for me. Because as long as I can get to that table, I'll have my peace."

Up All Night

Truck Stop

Jubitz never closes. It's a city unto itself, with barber, motel, gift shop, free showers, and twelve acres of big-rig parking. The restaurant has cushy red leatherette booths, phones at every table, perky, thin-boned waitresses, and a menu featuring four-egg omelets and fourteen-ounce steaks. Club 307, on the second floor above the convenience market, offers a place for truckers to hang out: there's a three-screen video arcade, computer hook-ups, a fax machine, and video games. The Ponderosa Lounge has had live music every night for the last thirty years. Jubitz advertises itself as "What a Truck Stop Should Be."

At the fuel lanes, Raymundo Somilleda, twenty-four, is swing shift assistant manager. At 11:00 p.m., he stands on the elevated platform behind the fuel counter, from where he can survey the convenience market, the deli, and the fluorescent island of fuel pumps outside. Clean-cut and bright eyed, he wears an olive green baseball cap with *Jubitz* stitched in white on a red oval.

Because Raymundo Somilleda is from outside the culture—his family roots are in Spain and he attended university as an architecture student in Mexico City—he is outside most of the mythology about truckers that shows up on the movie screens and juke boxes of the USA.

When he first started working at Jubitz, he had no ready translation for *bobtail, C-store, dead head, reefer, smokey,* nor any jargon he hears used by truckers over the fuel desk CB; he had no idea that truckers were a reliable source of rides and bennies back in the sixties, before trucking companies implemented "no-hitchhikers" policies and Benzedrine was regarded as *speed*; and he'd certainly never heard Bill Kirchen sing "Mama Hated Diesels" on Commander Cody's 1972 hit single. Raymundo Somilleda wasn't even born until 1975.

But he rapidly picked up on one important trademark of the clan: "They are really loyal. You can tell by the CB, they will help each other."

▲

129

Over at the Ponderosa Lounge, Glenn Stevens, a Melton Truck Lines driver out of White Castle, Louisiana, states it even more strongly: "I could go out there to that CB and get on the radio and say somebody was in trouble and you wouldn't *believe* how many truck drivers would come. You wouldn't *believe.*"

In three years of driving, this is only Glenn's second time in Portland. He goes to New York a lot, and figures he's driven his 1999 Kenilworth into Canada fifteen times. "I pull a flatbed, usually lumber or steel," Glenn says in his soft Louisiana drawl. "Melton is strictly a flatbed operation. I haul lumber into Canada, and they turn around and give me lumber to haul back. Honestly! I've pulled 2x4's into Quebec and they've loaded me up with 2x4's coming back. It's nothing but a money thing."

On his current run, Glenn loaded in Phoenix Monday evening. He drove 1,250 miles hauling two crates that had accidently been left off somebody else's load. "On a forty-eight-foot trailer, it took up about four feet of space," Glenn says. "It was some machinery going to a glass company.

"I arrived about eight this morning [Wednesday] to unload. I parked my truck, I took a shower, I went in and ate lunch, I went and took a nap in the truck. Then I came over here and the band was setting up."

A short, powerfully built man in tooled boots, Glenn has already been out on the floor, swing dancing, first with a forty-something blonde in a yellow dress and then, on the next number, with the woman she's sitting with. But when the country band—it's always a country band—begins playing the frantic licks from "Dueling Banjos," featured in the film *Deliverance*, he sits back down.

"I love seeing the country and meeting different people. I talk to anybody I see. I love it. The only thing I don't love is I'm away from my wife.

"But I never made money like I'm making now. I make forty-two hundred, forty-three hundred dollars a month—and I'm doing everything by the book."

▲

"I drove a truck a couple times." Raymundo speaks English fluently, with a Mexican accent and few grammatical irregularities. "A few years ago, I drove one of my friends' trucks, one of those big trucks. Just enough to see what it's like. I also worked for a company—before Jubitz—where we used to bring all kind of furnitures, so I used to drive a moving truck. You don't need a CDL to drive those kind of trucks. Sometimes I'd [think about] getting my commercial driver license 'cause I was driving truck, but then I thought, well, it's a tough job and right now I'm single, I don't have anyone, but sometime

I will. I mean, you have to leave your family for days, weeks, or even months to go to work. Even though you get a lot of money and it pays good, you have to sacrifice these things, and I didn't want to do that."

At Jubitz, Raymundo works from 3:30 in the afternoon until 12:30 in the morning and then goes home to his mother and brothers.

"The system that Jubitz has is that the beginners go to graveyard shift and then you go to a better shift. Of course there's seven graveyards—seven days, so somebody's got to cover those. I had two twelve-hour graveyard shifts and three swing shifts, and now I'm working five swings."

"It's a whole different world at night," Raymundo says. "It's like black and white. The truck drivers, the way they treat you, the way they talk to you. It's a whole different thing.

"Ten hours, I think, is the maximum haul. They can be driving legally without stopping to rest for a lot of hours. When they get some place all they want to do is get the best service they can. Jubitz teaches each one of the employees how to understand the drivers' way of life. We can't *feel* what they feel, but we have to be able to *understand* how they feel."

Truckers arrive tired, dirty, and hungry, their fuel tanks empty and their ashtrays full. Their cabs are littered with trash they've accumulated on the road—drink cups and gum wrappers, newspapers and napkins—and their clothes are ready for the washing machine. It is Jubitz's task—and therefore Raymundo's—to keep the truck stop clean in the face of this onslaught.

He keeps it spotless.

"I'm in charge of a group that's called Quality Assurance, QAD. One of my jobs is to take care of the cleaning crew, make sure they do the job, they have the right cleaning tools, they come in on time.

"I have a QAD person making sure all the restrooms in the fuel lane are clean, all the floors are mopped. I have another person just making sure the building station is clean.

"One of the most attractive things from Jubitz are showers. I mean they're not huge but they're big enough. We have eleven showers and we have a team that takes care of the shower cleaning. They've got to be clean all the time.

"My other job is to make sure the customers get right service. Most of my time at work I spend behind the fuel desk, behind the retail sales counter." His staff sells diesel and deli items, and Raymundo is there if they need help.

"Last month we sold around a million gallons of fuel. We have three cashiers and a lane attendant to make sure the pumps are clean all the time, change the garbage out there, make sure the lot is clean. Because the fuel lanes is a place with high potential to have an accident, we have someone out there twenty-four hours cleaning the pumps. We have eleven pumps. Sometimes they are all full and there's trucks lined up behind each other, especially during the day. It only takes a few minutes to fill up those tanks since the pumps are really fast. So we're trying to be the most safe but sometimes it's hard when you're this busy.

"Some of the drivers who get to the truck stop, the first thing they do is get fuel, make sure they have their tanks full, and then if they have to wait for a load sometimes they stay overnight, maybe two nights, until they get a load to go somewhere else. Sometimes they have to sleep, and they just find a spot to park and relax, have some coffee, a breakfast or lunch or dinner, whatever. They relax and stay there for a while until they have enough rest and they can get going.

"Right now, because we're remodeling, we have, I would say, around a capacity of three hundred spaces for trucks back there. But we have another parking lot, overflow parking lot, that should hold around a hundred fifty more spaces. And sometimes we are all full."

Truckers whose companies don't have their own computerized load tracking system will check the DAT Freight Matching system upstairs at Club 307 to find their next load.

"It doesn't cost anything to them," Raymundo explains. "They just go over there to check if there's a company which is interested to get a driver to get a load to some other places. It says a phone number for them to call. So all the drivers stop by to see that."

Club 307 is also part of Raymundo's domain. "They can drink beer up there, eat popcorn, relax and watch TV or watch movies. It's free. We have a list of all the movies, they can look at it, and then we play them on the video projectors. We try to get the latest ones. There's video games, pinball, poker machines, lottery. They socialize. They can have their coffee or cappuccino, and of course they're going to meet drivers."

At Jubitz, drivers can have their loads checked 24/7. "We charge $6.50 for weight, and they get a free re-weigh every time they have to re-weigh within twenty-four hours. During the day, we have a person at the scales. After 7:00 p.m, we close the scalehouse and we handle the scales from the fuel desk on the truck stop side. We have a camera and a CB at the fuel desk. That's the way we communicate with them to let them know their weight."

The scalehouse opens up again at five in the morning. "If they're leaving town, they want to get out very early," Raymundo points out, "like when there's no traffic out there."

In the fuel lane C-store, where most of the truckers wear boots and cowboy hats, Raymundo helps a woman driver who's just parked her eighteen-wheeler and wants to take a shower. A pack of cigarettes are visible in the front pocket of her red shirt, and she, too, wears a cowboy hat.

"There's a lot of women drivers out there," Raymundo says. "Maybe 30 percent. Maybe I exaggerate, but a lot. Maybe 20 percent. I see African American drivers all the time: most of the black drivers are young. Asian, quite a few, but I see more Mexican drivers than Asian."

Raymundo fits in a lunch break whenever he can. "Sometimes I don't take it. Usually I like to bring my own food because I like certain food that we don't have in the store. Of course, Mexican food—*tacos* or *torta* or *chiles rellenos* or beans. You know, we always have to have beans. I reheat it in the microwave.

"Somilleda is a Spanish name," Raymundo explains. "There's not many of us. If there's a Somilleda, that would be my family. They pretty much all come from the same little town in Hidalgo. It's called Xoté, Hidalgo, and it's just a *ranchería*—I would say no more than three or four hundred people. No, not even that, maybe two hundred people."

His family had moved to Mexico City by the time Raymundo was born, though they've stayed in close contact with Hidalgo.

"I still have family there. As a matter of fact I'm going to visit this year, and spend a couple of weeks over there, at Christmas.

"My dad immigrate to the States twenty years ago. I was four years old. He would come back to Mexico and I would see him for a few weeks in Christmas. He was bringing money home.

"Sometimes it's the only way you can survive with what's happening in Mexico, with the situation that is going over there. And, you know, having four kids, my brothers and me, it was hard to feed all the family. A lot of people come to the States to work and get enough money to survive and support family in Mexico.

"I went to the college in Mexico. I took classes at UNAM [Universidad Nacional Autónoma de México] in architecture. In Mexico the college is free. Books are not free, food is not free. So I had to work. And in order to do my homework, I would have to quit my job 'cause I couldn't handle it. Some day in my life, sometime in the future, I would like to continue with the same classes, maybe graduate. I love to draw pictures.

"My family is here now. I've been in the United States three and a half years almost. My brothers and my mother are here. I have three brothers; I'm the second oldest. We immigrate here to California. My dad lives in Salinas. He was staying in the same place for a long time. My dad drives a caterpillar, one of those tractors."

Raymundo's father had gotten legal residency under the 1986 amnesty, and because of him, the family could get papers. "When I immigrate here, I came with papers and that's something that I really had to thank my dad. That he had dealt with that. A lot of people can't get papers, and it's hard. I mean, you can work but you're always at risk, every day. You are so scared.

"I live there for about half a year, in Salinas, California. Salinas is a small place, rural. It's getting bigger and bigger, but the kind of jobs is all agriculture, and I don't like that. I'm a city boy. I mean I like to be in the city. So I look for something different, being in an environment that I like."

Raymundo learned about Portland through some friends, moved up here with them, and had rented an apartment and was working within a couple of weeks. After a few months at a job he didn't like, he was hired at the truck stop.

"At Jubitz, I started hourly and I started from the very bottom. Three years ago. My first job was pumping gas. Then I worked as a janitor for a few weeks, maybe a month, and then I moved up to deli cashier. From deli cashier I went up to what they call scalemaster.

"I was taking classes, doing my homework, reading. That stuff you can do because you are just sitting in a small office just by yourself. I took some classes at PCC Cascade. I took some ESL—English as a Second Language—classes. I still like to read, that's how I improve my English. I like *National Geographic*, computer magazines, all kinds of stuff.

"Anyway, we established our home, me and my brothers. They all live in my house. One of them is a forklift driver, he's a what-do-you-call it, night shift loader for Portland Bottling. The oldest one is a retail manager at Napa Auto Parts.

"My youngest brother is a student. He is taking classes at PSU. We are helping. He works, I mean, he's got a scholarship. Basically, if he gets good grades and he's doing good at school, he's got his tuition paid for four years. He's studying to be a graphic designer. He had a chance to go to high school and didn't have to worry about going to work.

"I didn't have the chance, right? But it doesn't mean that I cannot do it; I can *still* do it. It might take me a little longer. So, maybe some day."

Out on the roadway, a big semi can be heard, gearing down.

"I'd like to mention that Jubitz gave me an opportunity to improve my English, to have a better job, to do things that I wasn't doing. They gave me the opportunity to be what I am.

"At Jubitz they have that thinking—that you can always have the opportunity to do something better—and improve."

Up All Night

On the Door at Montage

At midnight under the eastbank pillars of the Hawthorne Bridge, in a district of old warehouses, there is a cluster of people on the sidewalk in front of Le Bistro Montage. Some are on their way out: they carry aluminum foil sculptures of swans, flowers, and helicopters, Montage's distinctive way of packaging leftovers; most are waiting in line to get in.

Inside, the large open L-shaped room is casual and loud. The racket comes from clattering dishes, piped-in jazz, customers shouting at each other to be heard, and waiters yelling "SHOOTER!" every time someone orders a raw oyster in a shot glass.

The eclectic menu ranges from expensive Bordeaux wines to a Spam-and-pesto omelet. The house specialty cocktail is a Bloody Manson, a standard Bloody Mary ingeniously garnished with Spam. Frog legs, crawfish, catfish, vegan gumbo, and a dozen jambalayas constitute the Cajun section of the menu; in pastas there are a dozen linguines and ten different varieties of mac and cheese.

From a mantel-height reception desk near the front door, manager Debora Doell directs traffic—chic little black dress, black cotton bobby socks, sturdy black shoes, and a ballpoint pen behind her right ear. At forty, Debora Doell has great attitude, delivery, and vocal range, and can achieve surprising effects by going from a whisper to a shout in the same sentence. With straight brown, shoulder-length hair and grey eyes, she's a plain woman whose great wit and animation draw people to her.

"Since we *don't* take reservations, people are *really* pushy. And I'll tell you what, I've met some of the biggest morons of my life at that door. They might not be morons in any other part of their life, but as soon as they walk through the door of the Montage, they turn into indignant morons.

"That is the one thing that I will never understand to the day I quit here or whatever I do. *'We were waiting for over an hour. Why?'* What am I supposed to say to that? I mean, seriously. 'Uh, because there's all these other people waiting and uh, I don't have a table for you and, guess what? There's a million other restaurants in this city where you *don't* have to wait at all.' And when

135

I say this, it's the truth, right? Isn't it the truth? And then they go, 'You don't have to be such a *bitch* about it.' Okay.

"You have to learn how to talk to them and control them in the best way possible and not *try* to offend them by being really blatant and up front, but in the interim I usually offend most people. I do my job like I did my job mainly in New York City and people out here can't seem to understand. They think I'm just being a blatant bitch to them. And I'm really not. I'm just trying to get them a table as *fast* as I possibly can, because *that is* my job.

"Montage seats about 125-30, and I usually probably get about 160 to 175 in here, on weekends especially. Plus all the people that are just standing around waiting. We open the door [at 6:00 p.m.] and most of the time on weekends I fill the restaurant within the first fifteen minutes. And then we're busy up until nine or ten. And then there's a little bit of a lull, and then we get pretty busy around eleven again. And then there's kind of a lull again, maybe at one or something, and then we'll get hit for the bar rush.

"On Friday and Saturday early we try to do somewhat more of a fine dining atmosphere for these people, but other than that, it is sort of like a café style, where we really want to turn and burn 'em, because we don't *have* a very expensive menu. And for my waiters to make *real* money, they *have* to get them in and out. *Averaging*, during the week, they're going to walk with probably anywhere from like a hundred to a hundred and fifty. You're going to take *in*, obviously, much more than you walk with. The waiters are very generous: they tip out really nicely to their bussers, because their bussers are busting ass for them.

"The manager needs to be here fifteen minutes before we open the door to make sure everything's set. The two bussers come in and set up the dining room and they have fifteen minutes to set it up on the weekdays. So I go around and make sure it's all *ready* to go. And then I do my little thing, I pull the waiters' packets for them and I get like matches out and all that little crap. And then I open the door.

"I am the dining-room manager but I also kind of override into the kitchen, too. Other than Daris [Ray] who ran that kitchen, there's never really been since him a kitchen manager. Nobody can seem to know how to *control* the kitchen. There are a lot of young testosterone-filled boys who are uncontrollable. I *try* to keep out of it basically. But I've had more say-so in that kitchen than any other person that has managed in there, only because I open my mouth, basically. I mean they all run to me a lot because they know I *will* open my mouth because they're too *scared* to open their mouth sometimes. Although, I don't know why because they all have big mouths anyway. But I am the mother figure.

"It has always been a male-dominated atmosphere, and I totally understand why. But it is a highly *aggressive* establishment. We're all *incredibly* aggressive people. And you don't last long here unless you are.

"It may sound mean, but we *are* like a little club. If I hire somebody and if they *truly* are not working out, they get the picture pretty fast. I've interviewed maybe one or two people in the five years I've been managing here. I go by hiring friends of employees. That's the other kind of clique we've gotten into, but it's much easier. And even at that sometimes they haven't worked out. But every time I tried to hire somebody from the outside, they truly *don't* work out. But I could see how it would be hard for somebody to come in here that didn't know anybody, because *we are family*. Truly very close-knit. I mean I see all these people every single day. We hang out with each other, we go do *everything* with each other.

"People *always* want to come to work. They *love* their job here and rarely are people sick, we're a pretty healthy crew. People come hungover, people come with the sniffles, cause it's a really *fun* place to work. It truly is. We have a really good time.

"Our restaurant, it's not real *technical* at all. And we've kept it that way on purpose. We've kept it like, yes, we have a computer that we put all our stuff into, but it's not the kind that spits shit out into the kitchen or the bar. We still do everything by hand. And in the beginning, when I first started working here, we didn't even have the computer to put all the merchandise in to add it up. Those waiters were adding their tickets up manually. But that was kind of a joke, 'cause I think we ended up probably losing a lot of money that way.

"Anyway, it all automatically works. I am *here* just as a control factor, just to make sure everything is kept at a level that it should be kept at, basically. But it *runs* as a *machine*.

"Basically you shut it down just like you open it up. It's kind of like you put-the-butter-back-in-the-cooler, you put-the-creamers-into-the-kitchen. 'Don't put the milk into the jug, you guys, you don't put the cream back into the jug, remember that. We're not saving the cream today.' Things like that. You put all the booze away and lock it up, you tear down all the tables, you put all the chairs up. It's pretty simple.

"Wednesday and Thursday we shut the door at two o'clock. And I'm here doing all the counting out til 2:30, 2:45. And then, depending on *when* all the people get out, *that's* how late I will be here, depending on the last customer that leaves. Friday we close the doors at *four*, so I'm done around *five*.

"Like I've been told this many times by this *one* guy that waits for me, he's from Albuquerque, and he said that he's never, ever, ever worked with a manager like me. Because I'm not *a micromanager*. I guess I'd never actually really heard that term before.

"I'd managed before. I managed a restaurant in New York and I managed a few hair salons along the line, and I not only learned from just prior management, but I learned from people managing *me* and the people that *I* thought that were really awful managers and did things that were just *so unnecessary*, that made you basically not *want* to do your job.

"And so, I just took it from there. I try to show them that I would do just about anything that *they* would have to do—although I'd never wait at a table here, that's *not* my job. But I'm not *above* getting out there and helping them when they need help. Like if it's really, really busy, getting out there and helping the bussers. Or if like the last waiter that's on is all alone, if he got really slammed, no I'm not *above* taking a couple tables' orders for him, you know, going around and taking drink orders or whatever.

"But the thing is, if someone's doing something *wrong*, first of all, I'm not going to present it to them until after the shift, you know, unless it's something that's ruining everything. Whereas *I have* been approached in a job before by a manager, like *right* in the middle and just telling me off! And like what does that *do* for you for the rest of your shift? Basically, you *hate* them, and you hate the job and *you* don't want to do it, you know? So I try the best I can.

"I have a big work ethic. I was brought up by Depression [-era] parents. They told me, 'You need to work.'

"I came from *north Portland* and went out [of the neighborhood] to LaSalle, a very upper-class Catholic High School. They truly looked at us like 'Oh north Portland, you got to be either a drug addict or a slut.' I started in '74 and North Catholic had burned down in '70 or that would have been where I would have gone, 'cause it was right down the street from us. Anyway, there was an abrupt break when I left the *door*, in 1978, but I'm really happy that my parents insisted I keep going.

"I worked at a fast-food restaurant in high school, and then right when I got out I went and applied at this *finance company* and got the job. It was called Capital Financial Services. And I was doing reception and then I was starting to be a loan officer. But it was boring.

"I've had so many jobs that it's ridiculous. I can like scramble through them like back and forth, but I mean this is the longest salary I'd ever had in my life, let's put it that way. I was in the hair industry for like ten years. I managed and did that reception stuff, but I do know how to cut hair, just from being in the industry for so many years. I did it here and then when I moved to New York I worked at Bumble and Bumble, which is one of the major hair salons there.

"I moved to New York in '85 because, first and foremost, I needed to get out of Portland, I needed to experience other culture. I was doing performance art and we'd sort of exhausted our circuit out here, going up and down the coastline. Like, really exhausted, like being kicked out of clubs and asked never to come back. And so I was like, 'Okay, if I'm going to experience other culture, *obviously*, this is the place.' I really only planned to be there for two years, get it out of my system. Because I realized from even the first visit there that it was a city that was going to take a lot away from you if you weren't really, really strong. But, I was there for six years.

"I have Graves' disease. It's a thyroid dysfunction. I lived with it for like nine months before I was diagnosed. What happened was I came back here one summer, I went and took some film courses at the Film School, and then I realized that I couldn't handle not living in New York: I had to go back. So I went back in like September or October, after that summer, and things just started falling apart rapidly. It's a little bit like Alzheimer's and a little bit like diabetes if there was no remedy, all that stuff. Your body just starts going way haywire physically and then you're emotionally just a wreck and then your mind starts going on you. I mean I was in dementia a number of times.

"I didn't come back here till March, so I was there like five months or whatever. And I called my parents a number of times and I didn't let on at first. I would call and just like start being kind of hysterical on the phone and start crying and stuff. Then I'd hang up on them. Finally I did just call one day and I told my dad, I said, 'I *don't* know what's wrong, I think I'm losing my mind basically and I need to come home.' I was all messed up. I couldn't even pack myself up to get back, so he had to fly out and pack me up and then we sent all my stuff and we got a drive-away and drove back across the country together.

"I started doing PR work for this woman in this *tiny* little florist shop downtown. My dad is a brilliant gardener, so I've always been around flowers. Then I left her and I just kept going from shop to shop. As I learned all I could learn from that shop, then I'd go to the next one. I learned from this woman who is a really brilliant floral designer with my second shop—she does a lot of Victorian-type stuff. And *then* I went on to Jacobsen's which was another shop where the woman that headed up there was Japanese. So I had two really good influences.

"I just walked into Montage one day 'cause I was doing floral design and I worked at Papa Hayden. I had my restaurant thing to back me up because you don't make all the money in floral design …

"I'd only set foot in Montage *maybe* four times before I was hired here. But I just walked in one day and it was like two o'clock in the afternoon and I was like, 'I put in a resume like a week ago, and I was just wondering if you remember who I am?'

"It was Jon [Beckel, the owner] and his manager at the time sitting there. So I said, 'Listen, I want to work your door. I worked in New York. I've worked doors, I've worked club doors, I've worked restaurant doors, blah, blah, blah. I'd love to work here.' And I said, 'That's *all* I want to do. I don't want to wait tables, I don't want to cook, I don't want to do any of that stuff.' I said, 'The only other thing is if you want to like give me a piece of the *pie*, I'll take that, but other than that I just want to work your door.'

"So Jon looked at me and said, 'Ooooh, okay.' He's like, 'We really *do* need somebody to work the door.'"

▲

"One thing I just did for the first time in five years here, and I felt like a big shithead, basically—I forgot to seat somebody. They were on my list like *way up here*, and I'd already turned the whole thing over and gone on like *a couple rows* over here, and—this was just this last Saturday or Friday—and the woman had been *standing there* and I was just *oblivious* to her, and she looked at me and she goes, 'We have really been here over an hour.' Over an hour is not unusual on a Saturday, but I looked at her and I was like, You *have* been here way too long. And I was like, 'What was your name?' and I looked it up and she was way back there *not crossed off*—'cause I cross them off as I go. She was way back on the list, with all the crossed-off people, and she was not crossed off and I'm like, *Oh, my God*, so I took them right to a table, sat them down—it was them and their two children—I sat next to the woman and I go, 'You know what? I feel really awful. I feel really, really like the worst I've felt ever in this job. 'Cause I've never done this before.' She looked at me and she was like, 'You know what?' she goes, 'Shit happens.' And I was like, She's okay! She's a nice woman! She's cool! So I bought them a bottle of wine. But see, on the other *hand*, that could have been somebody who would have bit my head off. It could have totally gone the other way.

"We get lots of kids. Which I love, too, because it's actually fun for kids 'cause it's so fast paced. They're like, Wow. Although I get angry with parents who let their children run around in there. When I went out with *my* parents:

once to the bathroom, *twice* was pushing it. *You know what I mean, though?* It's like if you really had to go twice, well it's *likely* you were going to do something else.

"We get the basketball players, we get the politician here and there, we get the newscaster here and there. The one thing I'm most proud of though is the percentage of African Americans eating in the restaurant. That's what makes me the happiest, especially having been born and bred here and knowing how segregated this city has always been. Every week it's like African Americans come more and more and feel more and more comfortable in our establishment. And I seat the punk rocker next to the old granny and then I see them like getting along like they've been old friends forever.

"The first word that usually comes to mind is it's *eclectic*. We want everybody to come here, first of all, as far as clientele. And that's what the whole atmosphere is like, that's obviously the word *montage*, that's what it means, it means a collage. I don't know the *exact* meaning, 'cause it is a French word.

"Obviously a lot of youth comes after like a certain hour. Like from eleven on, it's pretty youth-oriented, although there's the taxi cab guys, there's the guys who are doing whatever they're doing down in that industrial area late at night. They'll stop by.

"We don't get our share of cops. I think mainly the cops and the ambulance drivers probably get a *little* scared off from us because they do see lines, they do see packed-out house and they've got to do their stuff fast. Although I told a number of cops, I said, 'If you come in, if I seat you at the counter, you're going to be served within ten minutes.' But they don't realize how *fast* we really are. And I said, 'And also, you guys can get things to go anytime you want. That's like five minutes.' But I think that they're a little sketchy about us.

"We *don't* bend over backwards for *anybody*. I mean one time some *actors* entourage called up like, 'If we come in with like ten people can we be seated right away?' I'm like, 'No.' Basically, truly, flat out, if the president of the United States wanted to come into *that* restaurant on a Saturday night, he would have to wait like everybody else. I'm sorry! He would. It's the only way we *can* work here or we just start pissing people off *more* than we already do.

"But I also love the fact that the people who work here, we *do* inflict ourselves. Like if you've ever sat at the counter here, you *have* to listen to that kitchen. And they're not holding back much. They're using profanity, and they're talking about shit you may not want to hear about. But I kind of like that because *this is the real world, people.* You know, it *is* nice to go to a place where everybody's very quiet and pleasant and talking about very nice things all the time. That's wonderful, that's great, whatever. But you know it's not the real world 'cause the real world is really people who—I mean even the nicest person, even the nun out there, has probably gotten a little *jacked up* at times and said some things. You know what I mean, though? I like that. I like that you're in their face and that they have to see that this is what reality is, you know? And if you don't like hearing *fuck*, don't come here, seriously. There's a million restaurants here per capita, you don't have to be here. Nobody asked you to come."

The door to the street swings open and two more departing customers shoulder their way past hungry people waiting to get in.

Up All Night

In Perfect Silence

...I wander'd off by myself,
In the mystical moist night-air, and from time to time,
Look'd up in perfect silence at the stars.

Walt Whitman
"When I Heard the Learn'd Astronomer"

Up All Night

Star Party

Others may promise you the universe, but we deliver.
Rose City Astronomer's message machine

At 7:20 p.m., on a night in mid-October, Bob McGown pulls his brown LandCruiser off SE 174th Avenue in front of Lynch Wood Elementary and steers around to the south side of the building, where several cars are parked. He turns off his headlights so as not to ruin the dark adaptation of the people who are already viewing, and drives slowly across the athletic field.

Thirty feet from where McGown comes to a stop, Rick Kang has been letting kids take pictures of the night sky with a CCD (charged couple device) camera hooked up to a six-inch telescope. Kang has driven up from Eugene, where he does educational outreach for the Pine Mountain Observatory, based in Central Oregon. His laptop sits on a cafeteria table that someone has dragged out to the athletic field, and around him a crowd of fifth graders and their parents are viewing the screen with its captured images of the sky.

McGown opens the back of the brown LandCruiser and begins hauling out the things he'll need to set up his enormous Dobsonian telescope. McGown's a big guy, six foot four, with thick chestnut hair and heavy sideburns. He wears jeans and a warm jacket, which hangs open to reveal PALOMAR MOUNTAIN, printed on his black t-shirt. By day a master electrician, McGown is by night an active member of Rose City Astronomers (RCA), Portland's popular amateur club. When Rick Kang requested that RCA send a second telescope to tonight's star party, McGown happily responded. This is exactly what McGown, forty-five, loves doing.

First, McGown unfolds a lightweight aluminum camp table with benches attached on both sides. This will serve as a work surface on which to keep track of lenses, filters, and tools. He spreads a canvas on the grass and on that he sets the big rocker box—that is, the base of the telescope which, as the name implies, "rocks" on bearings that allow the big telescope to be maneuvered up and down and side to side. Inside the rocker box nests the box containing the primary mirror.

144

McGown clamps eight truss poles to the rocker box. The poles stick up six feet in the air, forming a framework for the tube. As he circles this framework, tightening up all the clamp blocks, he chats with the people who have gathered around him.

"It's kind of light polluted," he tells them, "but we'll see something." It's a cold, clear night and dark at the spot he is standing, but porch lights and lit windows can be seen around the periphery of the athletic field, and there are half a dozen street lamps a block away.

In addition to showing up at star parties with his telescope, McGown is RCA's official light pollution rep, which means that he lobbies city lighting engineers to point street lights toward the earth, where they're needed, and not up into an already light-polluted sky. In this work, McGown is aided by statistics and printed material from the International Dark Sky Association, which counts migrating birds and newly hatched sea turtles among those whose interests are best served by darkness.

An object comes out of the back of the LandCruiser that looks like a bass drum in a canvas case: this is the cage, containing the secondary mirror. McGown pulls out an eight-foot aluminum ladder, custom made for astronomy, with an extra-wide stable base, and closely spaced steps with a non-slip tread. Opened and standing, the ladder has the graceful shape of the Eiffel Tower.

By the time he's up on the ladder and clamping the cage to the top of the trusses, all the fathers have strolled over to his part of the field. They stand there watching, making dark burly shapes barely visible against the night sky.

"What does something like this cost?" one of the fathers asks.

"As much as a good speedboat," McGown says. The man looks thoughtful as the arithmetic sinks in, and McGown adds, "I got it used."

Fully assembled, the trusses wrapped in canvas, McGown's Dobsonian is an imposing black cylinder, towering over the athletic field, with a twenty-inch aperture aimed at the sky. Some of the kids come over now to have a look. "Cool," one of the fifth graders says.

McGown works for a few more moments in silence. "We've assembled it," he announces. "Now we're going to collimate it."

As he tips the big tube at a 45-degree angle toward the target moon, he can't help admiring his own telescope. "Isn't it amazing how smooth the action is?" he asks no one in particular.

To collimate a reflector telescope, the secondary mirror (on the sky end) must be positioned just right over the primary mirror (on the ground end), an operation which is done by looking, adjusting knobs, and looking again. McGown asks one of the fathers to help turn knobs, and the man calls him "Sir."

"There should be a black shroud here," McGown says. He slips a big canvas sleeve over the trusses, turning the skeletal cylinder into a solid black tube. "The shroud is simply to prevent light pollution," he explains.

Impatient with the delay, one ten-year-old boy runs off into the darkness, shouting back over his shoulder, "It's time to hit some girls."

"I don't think so," his father says. Laughter and squeals are heard from the direction of the monkey bars.

Satisfied with the alignment of the optics, and oblivious to the departing boy, McGown adds an aperture stop, a black disk which fits over the twenty-inch sky-end opening, shutting it down to a three-inch viewing hole. "We put in the aperture stop because the moon is so bright," he explains.

Now, at 7:55, thirty minutes after McGown parked the car, people begin looking through his big telescope at the moon, which is a fat crescent hanging in the southwest.

"Isn't that amazing?" says the man standing at the eyepiece, which is mounted near the front end of the scope. A line forms behind him, but he shows no sign of moving.

"There is no dark side of the moon," McGown points out to the group, "only a far side."

Even the kids are quiet now, waiting their turn in line.

David Scharfenberg, the fifth-grade teacher whose students are here tonight, comes over to introduce himself. Mr. S., as the kids call him, has been working with Rick Kang at the CCD table up until this moment. Tall, gangly, and sincere, he shakes McGown's hand and thanks him for coming out with the big scope. Though he teaches all subjects to his class of fifth graders, he confesses that science is his favorite.

"Today the kids made constellations in class," he tells McGown. They splattered white paint on black paper and used a white marker to connect the seven biggest dots. Then they named their "constellations" and wrote stories about them.

"One boy figured he had made a seahorse, but didn't want to use such a common name," Mr. S. tells McGown. "So he asked the two Spanish-speaking boys in the class, and they came up with a name he liked better: *Cabellitos del mar.*"

Only two-thirds of David Scharfenberg's fifth grade class is here tonight, although all twenty-seven kids were invited. "They were required to bring at least one parent," Mr. S. says, shaking his head. "That's always kind of a limiting factor."

Sixteen people are waiting in line for the Dobsonian. "Don't bump the eyepiece," one of them says to the kid trying to get a look.

Now that the moon-viewing line is moving smoothly, McGown begins to give a naked-eye tour of the night sky to the people waiting in line. He points to Saturn coming up over the schoolhouse roof, but it turns out no one is as tall as he is, so only he can see it. Overhead, he points out the constellations Andromeda, Perseus, Cassiopeia, Lyra, and, on request, the bright white star, Capella.

A boy in a sweater cap taps McGown on the elbow. "How come we only look through that little hole?" he asks.

"'Cause if we used the whole telescope we'd get too much light," McGown explains. "See, this is a big telescope that was made for looking at galaxies." He puts on a UHC (ultra high contrast) filter and rotates the scope toward the east and the planet Jupiter, which is larger than all the other planets in our solar system put together.

One of the mothers is first up at the scope. A few moments after positioning her eye, she exclaims, "I can see four moons!"

"I go online and look at the Hubble," Mr. S. tells McGown. "They always have the astronomy picture of the day."

"Is that your little six-inch over there?" McGown asks him.

"No, that's Rick's," Mr. S. says. "I'm still saving for my telescope."

"Why don't you buy one like this, David?" one of the fathers asks the science teacher, teasing.

"Yeah, you could mortgage the school," McGown says, and he swings the scope to the big yellow planet, Saturn, now risen high enough above the schoolhouse to be seen. He looks through the eyepiece for a moment and adjusts the focuser knob. "One of the reasons Saturn's best perched for viewing now is that its rings appear sharply tilted," McGown explains.

As one of the fathers looks in the eyepiece, McGown points out the moon right next to Saturn. "That's Titan," he says. "Saturn's the one Cassini is going to."

The Cassini spacecraft had a controversial launch in October of 1997 when activists protested the use of generators that rely on plutonium oxide. Should Cassini have an accident, it could cause an environmental hazard of the first order.

"Wow!" the man at the eyepiece says. "How long does it take to get there?"

"About four more years," McGown says.

The next man steps up to the eyepiece. "And the moon is to the right?" he asks.

"Yes," McGown confirms.

"That's awesome. Genese," he calls to his wife, "you can see rings around it."

Genese looks through the scope, and the rest of the line takes a step forward.

McGown takes another peek through the eyepiece. "We're getting a little bit of turbulence here," he says, "because heat is rising off the asphalt roof of the schoolhouse."

He swings the scope around and tilts it so steeply that the eyepiece is eight feet in the air. "We're going to look at Andromeda next," McGown says. "That's a galaxy." After he focuses, the first viewer, a girl named Chelsea, climbs up the ladder.

"All the stars that you see here belong to the Milky Way Galaxy," McGown is saying. "And there are billions of other galaxies."

It's chilly tonight. Several of the fathers, after having a look at Andromeda, motion their children back to the car. "Let's see, what will we look at?" McGown asks himself aloud, oblivious to the departures. "M-15," he says decisively. "Let's look at M-15."

"What's M-15?" one of the fathers asks.

"It's a globular cluster with a compact core," McGown says, though the man still looks puzzled. "It's a breathtaking object and it has hundreds of thousands of very, very old stars."

The "M" designation means that it was one of the objects identified by the French astronomer, Charles Messier. His famed list of "Messier Objects" assigns a separate number to each of the 110 objects that he could see through his small telescope in the eighteenth century. A passionate comet hunter, Messier's purpose was to establish an inventory of the dim, fuzzy objects that are *not* comets because they kept intruding on his comet search. RCA gives awards to club members who have observed all 110 Messier objects.

"It's remarkable how many good astronomers in our club have never gotten their Messier certificate," McGown has commented. "They're busy on the computer all the time, indoors," is McGown's theory. He points out that NASA scientists have estimated that there are enough celestial images online to fill six thousand CD Rom disks. Within RCA, there are many other ways to get sidetracked as well, such as making telescopes, observing the sun, studying the weather, or astrophotography, to name a few.

At Lynch Wood Elementary, one man is still walking around exclaiming over the wonder of having seen Saturn with its rings. "It was just *so* clear," he says.

"They said it's supposed to drop down to 32 degrees tonight," someone says.

Two of the girls in the fifth-grade class are walking away from the field, evidently on their way home. Mr. S. calls after one of them, "Julie, Julie."

She stops and turns around. "Yeah?"

"Julie, I have a question for you," the science teacher yells.

"What?" she calls back across the field.

"How much further down the ballfield would you be if I hadn't stopped you?"

She stands still, baffled.

"The answer is: about where Michelle is," the teacher shouts, pointing to Julie's friend who's still trudging toward home. "Goodnight," he calls.

She calls back, "Goodnight, Mr. S."

Only a handful of people are left. "The first thing you do if you want to learn astronomy," McGown is explaining to a small group of listeners huddled in the chill, "is you learn the constellations. And then you just move around the sky, starting with the bright objects."

McGown focuses the Dobsonian on the Double Cluster. "This is a real pretty object," he says. "It's in Cassiopeia, off the flat arm."

Only Mr. S., his girlfriend, three dads, and one boy are left. Across the way, the six-inch telescope is disassembled, and Rick Kang is beginning to fold up the CCD camera and his computer.

"Cassiopeia is just very rich with open clusters," McGown is saying, unfazed by the dwindling numbers of people, the late hour, the cold.

Born in 1954, McGown went through the Portland schools in the era of Apollo. "I couldn't help but be excited about space and astronomy," he says today. "They'd take the TV right into our classroom when we were in the fifth and sixth grade. Sputnik was going over and it was really exciting then."

McGown's newest interest is the Mars Society, and especially their Devon Island Mars Arctic Research Station, which is north of Baffin Island. "They're putting a biosphere up there for potential Mars colonists to study what it would be like to live on Mars," he says with excitement. "My goal is to go up and stay in their biosphere."

He removes the UHC filter, and the reds and blues pop out in the Double Cluster. Six people take their turn climbing back up the ladder to see the reds and blues, and then McGown swings it back to Saturn, which is already higher in the sky. The man who loves Saturn hurries over to look through the eyepiece once again.

"Thank you, Mr. S. Goodnight," a child calls from somewhere in the dark.

"Dad, Dad, Mom's here," some child calls from the parking lot.

Now only the science teacher, Rick Kang, and two women are left.

"We've got this perfect sky tonight!" McGown declares. He swings the scope around again and sets it up for the Ring Nebula. Rick Kang looks through the eyepiece at the perfect grey smoke ring puffed into the sky.

A woman in a bulky parka asks to see one particular star. "I've always heard about Vega," she says.

McGown positions the telescope to show her the fifth-brightest star in the sky. She makes her way to the top of the ladder and lingers there, meditating on the distant blue sapphire above.

Finally, it registers with McGown that everyone else has gone. If this were one of the big RCA star parties, with one hundred plus telescopes set up, McGown and his colleagues would observe until dawn. Now he accepts the assistance of Rick Kang and David Scharfenberg, and in ten minutes they pack the big Dobsonian into the brown LandCruiser.

Reluctantly, McGown leaves the dark schoolyard and heads back toward the center of town, where streetlights and stop lights, lit billboards and buildings have all but extinguished the stars.

Up All Night

Awake at the Zoo

Blair Neuman works alone. Security guards and custodians are on the premises, but by the time she comes to work, at four in the afternoon, the day keepers have gone home. Alone she'll cover the entire sixty-four-acre zoo in the course of her ten-hour shift.

"In theory I'm responsible for the whole collection. I feel I need to check, to actually look at, every animal at least once."

Blair sprints along the paved paths wearing black leather workman's boots, her pager and radio dangling from her belt and a long mane of kinky black hair flying out behind her. "There are no short cuts," she points out. "I need a jet pack." Before sundown, wherever she goes, the ubiquitous peacocks, which live loose on the grounds, strut along the roadway or perch above her on a wall.

Blair's primary responsibilities are feeding the animals, making sure they are secured, and watching for any irregularities that may signal an animal is sick or in danger.

"Wild and exotic animals do an excellent job of hiding illness and injury," Blair says. Covering up any indication of weakness is a survival instinct, since a weak animal would be the likely target of a hungry predator going for the easy kill, or for hierarchical overthrow within the group. So for zookeepers, early detection of symptoms can be harder than one might suppose.

For detecting danger, Blair is especially attentive to sounds. "If a chimp's flipping out, I know what that sounds like," Blair says. "If it's an alarm call, I'll investigate, especially at a weird time of night. With the chimps, it could be like one chimp having a bad dream. When one goes off they all go off. But you never know. It could be an intruder stumbling into something and setting the animals off."

In summer, the gates close at six o'clock, but people are still on the grounds until seven, so for the first three hours of Blair's shift, she's limited in what she can get done. "The animals don't get fed before the zoo closes because it takes them off exhibit. I can kind of get away with doing some of the primates because they eat fairly quickly and stay on exhibit to eat, so I'm not really shutting them away."

Just around closing time, she feeds the mountain goats. Typically, animals are housed in an area that has three different compartments: the exhibit area, which is their most commodious space; an off-exhibit holding area, where they may be admitted to feed or to otherwise have privacy; and a keeper area, the backstage office with computer, refrigerator, and records on animal care. With few exceptions, Blair does not go into the animals' space, be it their exhibit or their off-exhibit holding area. "The keepers *do* go out with the mountain goats," Blair says, "but we just got a new male in—about two years old. I've heard day shift talking and I've gotten the impression that he would challenge them, so they don't necessarily want to go out with him."

Her procedure is to enter the keeper area, get the four bowls of grain, herbivore pellets, and alfalfa that have already been prepared by dayshift, and set the bowls in the goats' off-exhibit holding area. Then she raises a door between the two areas, rings a brass cowbell to summon them to eat, and then moves swiftly back into the safety of the keeper area as the goats head for the feed.

Blair's next stop is the lorikeets, who live in a walk-through, open-air aviary of wire mesh enclosing a leafy habitat full of jewel-colored birds. The blue-streaked lory is especially beautiful, bright scarlet with a single swipe of indigo. The smallest of the parrot family, lories are native to Australia, the South Pacific, and Indonesia. In the wild, they travel from tree to tree in noisy flocks; at the Oregon Zoo, they will fly down and land on a person's shoulder and drink nectar, which the zoo makes available in small cups. Because of this interaction and their rainbow-hued beauty, the lories are popular with the public. But now, since it is 7:00 p.m., Blair clears the last of the public out of the viewing area and locks the entrance to that walkway. Finally, she's alone with the animals.

"Every zookeeper's dream is to have a private zoo and keep the public away," Blair admits. "The reason I would prefer a 'visitor-free' zoo is due to the rude folks that come in and have no respect, the ones who throw things and yell at the animals to react." The summer evening Zoo Concerts can be problematic. "What I really don't like is the people who bring their kids because they're too cheap to get a babysitter. It's a long concert, the kids don't care, so they wander around. Having unattended children wandering around makes me very nervous.

"On the other hand," she acknowledges, "when people ask you intelligent questions, that's kind of cool."

In the marine life exhibit at the Steller Cove, she lets the otters have access to their off-exhibit pools. This is done from the walkway above, by cranking open the metal gate that divides their tank. Eddie the sea otter comes through first, climbs to the edge of the concrete pool, and rubs against the chain link, his long whiskers poking through. This is one of three animals that Blair will actually touch. She noogles his stomach with a knuckle. Thelma, the female otter, is swimming in an adjacent pool, ignoring the affections between Eddie and Blair.

In the Insect Zoo, Blair regards the glass tank of Madagascar Hissing Cockroaches with genuine disdain. They are the only zoo creatures that disgust her. Once she came in and found the tank's lid cocked and realized some of the roaches were loose. She replaced the lid and called security rather than search the room herself. Now she checks the heater, refills the humidifier, and makes sure the lids are secure on the tanks.

She locks the Pygmy goats in their barn, where they appear happy and relieved after a day on exhibit in the petting zoo. As she kneels to secure the doorway to the outdoor pen, one small goat sneaks up behind her and nibbles the radio hanging from her belt.

At the Alaska Tundra, the door to the keeper office is posted with a red "Danger" sign. Here and throughout the zoo, Blair opens and closes exhibit doors remotely from the safety of the keeper area, either on a manual pulley-and-counterbalance system or hydraulically.

This is the wolf area, home to Marcus and two females. Blair gives them access to their off-exhibit dens, and they come in and wheel around with yawning mouths full of impressive teeth. "I neurotically check every door," Blair says. "The first rule of zookeeping is don't trust anyone, including yourself." When she leaves, the three wolves race out to watch her go, leaping at the metal fence.

Contrary to what many people think, animals are not especially affected by a full moon. "I don't know if *any* of them are," Blair says. However, because humans tend to act out during a full moon, there are more police and ambulance sirens. "And if the wolves hear sirens it makes them howl."

Three musk ox chew placidly as Blair jogs past them, heading toward Africa.

"I don't really have a favorite animal," Blair says. "There are too many good ones." Having said that, she goes to feed an animal that makes her smile. Stinker, the Abyssinian Ground Hornbill, is a big glossy black bird, probably three feet long from tip of her crescent-shaped bill to the end of her tail. Blair puts down a dish of refrigerated dead mice for Stinker, then pulls the lever that opens the guillotine door to give her access to her off-exhibit area, where the food is. The hornbill steps delicately inside, her long eyelashes giving her the look of a coquette. She delicately picks up a mouse with the point of her bill, tosses it in the air and lets it fall into her open throat. "I sense that she likes to play," Blair says, "but I'm not really sure how to play with her."

Africa is a large area in the far southwest corner of the zoo, with several buildings and complicated, winding paths. Blair has often discovered a person or two down here, looking for the way out of the zoo. "It was embarrassing when I first started working," she explains, " 'cause I wasn't sure where the exit was either."

In the steamy building called African Rainforest, Blair opens the lid of a tank and mists a mossy exhibit of tiny orange mantella frogs. The size of a human thumb, they look plastic. Blair turns off two switches in a closet, pulls the pump plug, turns off lights and fans, and keeps moving.

It's not quite dusk yet when Blair arrives at the African Aviary. Two knee-high duikers, small antelope-like animals, live in here with the squawking, chattering birds, and Blair pulls out their bowls so as not to attract rodents in the night. From a high perch, a white ibis watches her pick up the dishes. A beautiful cattle egret glows white in the shadows of the leaves. Ducks stare into the pond.

In the mechanical room Blair turns off the waterfall for the swamp colobus exhibit. The sudden quiet is a cue for the African monkeys that their food is about to arrive. Blair gives them people-grade romaine lettuce, along with fruits and vegetables. "Nothing is too good for these animals," she points out. "No expense is spared."

The colobus is a long-tailed black and white monkey that appears to be wearing a white bearded skirt. In the roaring twenties, furriers used these monkey skins to trim fur coats; today deforestation is their major threat.

Outside, a big sleek rat stands on the concrete path ahead of Blair, not bothering to move. As she comes abreast of it, it lazily walks into the underbrush at the side of the road. It is plump and silky from the high-grade diet of pellets it steals from the animal collection. Despite an aggressive pest-control program, Blair says she's seen more rats than ever this year at the zoo.

In the hoofstock barn, Blair puts down kudu diet—three quarts of pellets, two portions of alfalfa flakes, one carrot, one apple, half a yam, and greens— then opens the door for the kudu moose to come into his stall, taking care to stay out of sight. The kudu moose does not like to be watched, not even a peek through the wooden slats of his stall.

Blair lets the two zebras, Frack and Citation, into their respective stalls, making sure to lock the access doors behind them. On her way out of the barn, Blair does peek at the kudu moose: he is elegant, fawn-colored with thin white stripes.

It's dark now as Blair makes her way through the densely planted grounds. "In a couple of areas it's kind of secluded," she says, "so if people broke into the zoo, I'd worry about that. But I have great run-away instincts, and I would know where I was going if I was fleeing from somebody."

To enter the primate area, Blair steps through a tray of disinfectant. Great care is taken to not bring in germs because the monkeys, chimps, and apes are vulnerable to human diseases.

It's easy for the keepers to feel a kinship with the primates.

"I remember once with the apes, I was trying to close them in for the night. It was a male and his girlfriend and daughter. There was a carton in the way, so I couldn't close the hydraulic door. It wouldn't close and *ping* properly, making it safe. So I just talked him through it, 'Go get that out of the way.' And it worked! I was absolutely communicating with that animal. Maybe he didn't know initially what I wanted, but he knew I wanted something. And he knew what the routine was."

The primate building is also home to a Burmese python named Goldie. In the wild, she's a rainforest dweller and more active at dusk and dawn. Already over ten feet long, she can grow up to twenty feet and two hundred pounds. Like so many of the animals Blair takes care of, pythons have declined in the wild because of habitat loss and poaching.

And now, with only an hour to go before her lunch break, Blair hurries through the next set of buildings, where she checks a very serious little pygmy owl that tours with the Zoo Teens program. She also gives bears access to their off-exhibit holding areas and inspects the trout water-filter system in the pump room for the Cascade Stream.

At the Center for Species Survival, she adjusts the room temperature and dumps old food pans. The public never sees this area, where sick animals receive special nursing, new animals are quarantined for observation before they enter population, and animals are brought to breed.

Blair pops into the back office of the mole rats, where she records the temperature and the humidity. Music blares from the radio behind their exhibit. "They are so sensitive to sound that the radio is kept on day and night so as to mask any other abrupt intruding sounds," Blair explains. "What they listen to just depends on the taste of the day keeper," she adds. Tonight the mole rats are listening to funk.

On her way back to the time-clock area, where she'll take her thirty-minute lunch, Blair stops at the tree kangaroos, turns out the lights, and lets down the big cloth blinds that screen them from the roadway. The adorable and popular Yowee, born over Mother's Day weekend 1999, is in a room with her mother, adjacent to her dad. She recently moved out of her mother's pouch where she lived for the first fourteen months of her life.

Nine-thirty and Blair's first rounds are over. She gets her lunch out of the big walk-in cooler where the penguins' zoo smelt is stored, puts her feet up on a desk and sits by herself reading day-shift reports.

▲

Blair, thirty-seven, was raised in Philadelphia. She majored in anthropology at Oberlin, though, as now she says, "I only like people in theory." In 1985, when she graduated, she had to figure out what she was going to do, trying to make up her mind between handicrafts and working with animals. "If I did the animal work," she reasoned, "I could probably at least make minimum wage, whereas I could actually starve to death if I did the crafts."

At the time, there were just two schools in the United States where she could learn to work with exotic animals. She applied to Moorpark College in Los Angeles, because she'd heard the Florida program was too easy. In twenty-four months she earned an Associate of Science degree in exotic animal training and management.

After three years at the San Francisco Zoo, Blair was officially hired at the Oregon Zoo on December 1, 1993. "There were two positions available, a rover position and a night position," Blair recalls. Today she's glad she made the choice she did, because her favorite part of the job is working alone at night. "And plus, I get to have a relationship with *all* the animals, whereas day people don't work in all the areas." She also likes the fact that she gets to—is required to, in fact—check in on any new babies born at the zoo.

After lunch, she pulls a hundred pounds of carrots, two large bunches of bananas, three big boxes of apples, along with a tray of refrigerated smelt out of the cooler, loads them on a dolly, and rolls them out to the loading dock. From there she transfers them into the back of the Mitsubishi, a little truck that the zookeepers use to transport food around the grounds. The last four hours of her shift, she'll travel in the Mit, along service roads that don't show up on any zoo map.

At the hippo and rhino barn she makes a food drop, and at the penguin exhibit, she stashes fish in the refrigerator. As usual, Mulchica, "the penguin ambassador," is waiting up for her, wide awake. She lets him into the kitchen area, stands over him and strokes his head and back. He hunkers down between her boots, loving it. "He's never mated," Blair says.

Sometimes she's found fifteen penguins loose in the keeper area. She figures Mulchica pushes open the glass door from the exhibit and lets the other penguins in behind him.

At 11:30, Blair reaches the elephants, which are the pride of the Oregon Zoo and have brought it international fame. Beginning with the birth of Packy in 1962, twenty-seven Asian elephants have been born at the zoo. This is actually Blair's third visit to the elephants: she came at six o'clock and at nine to feed. Now, she'll feed once again, and clean their area.

Upon arriving at the elephant barn, Blair is required to notify security. Since the largest male elephant is the size of a combine and has the heft of a boxcar, security wants to keep tabs on her when she's down here. A sharp odor assails her as she opens the door to the keeper area, half dung and half testosterone, which exudes from glands located near the temples on Rama, a towering teenager now in his first *must*. The word, which comes from the Hindi, means ruttish or intoxicated, and is used to describe the sexual frenzy of male elephants, which may last two months at a time.

A mouse scampers across the concrete floor. Blair says it's not true about mice and elephants: there's no chronic fear, as people believe. "Elephants don't see so well," Blair adds, "so they can be startled by the movements of mice."

Just now, there are three males and four females, the latter kept together, the males each in separate units. Blair runs fresh water in the trough for "the girls," as she calls them, and they rumble in acknowledgment, sometimes even flapping their ears. She's learned to distinguish between the various sounds the elephants make. "The rumbles are their good noise," Blair says. "There's a high-pitched squealing noise they do, an excitement-type noise which can go either way, something good happening or something scary going on. When elephants trumpet, it's like extreme excitement."

"The girls" consist of Pet, forty-five, a hairy, pigeon-toed elephant with bulging eyes; her daughter, Sung-Surin (whom the keepers call Shine), at seventeen, the largest female; Rose-Tu, five; and Chendra, the much-publicized six-year-old who arrived in November 1999.

Chendra had been taken into captivity after being shot while with her herd near a palm-oil plantation on the island of Borneo. The injury left her blind in the left eye, so she was not returned to the wild. On permanent loan from the government of Malaysia, she arrived in Oregon weighing half a ton and began gaining about forty pounds per week. Yams are her favorite food.

Blair changes into the rubber galoshes she will wear for swabbing out the elephant rooms. Because no two males can share the same space, nor can the females be put with any of the three males, Blair's system for moving the elephants from room to room is as complex as the old riddle about the man who wanted to move the fox, the goose, and the corn safely across the river. She puts down apples, yams, and carrots, then goes into a protected area where she can operate the hydraulic doors, letting Rama in with the food and closing the door behind him. Blair opens and closes all doors with great care. She remembers her predecessor telling her, "Be very careful in the elephant barn. Any mistakes you make here will be global, like CNN."

"As though the pressure weren't high enough!" Blair says, with a laugh.

There are two outdoor elephant yards, in addition to several high-ceilinged, dungeon-like rooms, with iron eyes screwed into the concrete walls in case restraints are needed. When Blair arrives, Packy, the largest, oldest male is in the front yard, Hugo is in the back, and Rama is indoors. When she is done, the front yard and the interior room will have been cleaned, and Packy's and Rama's positions switched: Rama will spend the night outdoors.

Blair uses a thirty-inch squeegee to clear dung and hay from the inside rooms, and a shovel to clean the yard. An elephant bolus is a huge cylindrical pellet, which can be as large as a human head. When woven through with hay, it has a golden hue. Normally it takes Blair an hour and forty-five minutes in the elephant area. It's her most sustained task and she finds it can be a meditation. In fact, on New Year's Eve, she timed her shift so that she could celebrate the millennium "picking up the biggest elephant turds in America" as the clock struck midnight.

The girls have been waiting in the front yard while Blair cleans their rooms, and now she has to move them back inside. She forks out bales of hay for them, liberally sprinkled with apples. Little Chendra was once knocked down by Shine, and she is sometimes shy about coming back indoors, so Blair has devised a trick: she takes a huge bucket of apples and cuts each apple into six or eight pieces. The big elephants come in and start picking up the apple pieces with their trunks, but since the pieces are so small, it takes forever. As the girls get absorbed with this task, little Chendra senses it's safe and sneaks in behind them.

Blair also gets Rama into the clean front yard by throwing down apples, but they are whole. Without pause, he picks each apple up in his trunk, doubles his trunk back underneath, and pops the apple into his mouth. It appears that he waits until he has a mouth full of thirty apples before he swallows. Then he rears his head, breathing in the night air, majestic in profile against the moon.

Blair leaves the area at 1:00 a.m., radioing security that she's safely out of the barn. Had they not gotten her call, they would be down there, troubled.

The last animal Blair moves indoors is a nine-year-old male Amur leopard. When Blair pulls up in the Mit, Frederick is pacing his thickly planted habitat. He has a yellowish coat and his spots are widely spaced rosettes with thick borders. Blair easily gets him inside with chunks of raw horsemeat, which he laps in a few quick gulps, and a huge joint of meat, which he takes to his indoor perch to play with.

Next door, his sister, Andrea, sits on a high perch, watching his arrival with wonderful feline indifference; only her long tail swings back and forth.

Named after the Amur River on the border of northeast China and southeast Russia, these leopards have also suffered from human encroachment and poaching. There are thought to be as few as sixty left in the wild and an estimated sixty-four in captivity in North America.

"I think there is value in having animals in captivity," Blair says, "though it may be just a feeble human effort since we're wrecking everything. Once they're gone, they're gone. I'd rather have the chance that some future utopia could be populated.

"Of course, zoos are supposed to educate people about these animals and their plight, thus making them want to help, but I feel the most important job of zoos is keeping a viable gene pool and the possible chance for these animals to thrive at some future time when *people* become more enlightened.

"I don't think I'm saving the world. Taking care of animals gives *me* personal satisfaction. I think every keeper wishes the world were such a way that you wouldn't need to have zoos. But people destroy habitat. With me, that's the critical thing: to save the habitat."

At the end of her shift, she will break down food boxes for recycling. The primate keeper, an old-timer with nearly thirty years here, has asked that she check the primate building every night just before she goes home. There was once a fire in the Philadelphia Zoo primate building, and he is haunted by the thought. Blair is glad to do this errand, for her friend and for the primates themselves. As she puts it, "Just about any keeper, including myself, would kill or die to defend these animals."

She walks through the night shadows to the center of the zoo. In the primate building, the lights are out. The mandrills are asleep, the gibbons are asleep, the howlers, chimps, and orangutans are asleep. Blair takes care to shield her big flashlight so as not to wake them. She stands there for a moment, sensing their presence as they, perhaps, sense hers. She is the safe one, the one who comes and goes in the dark. After a moment she leaves in silence, checking the door behind her.

Up All Night

Mr. Thomas at the Embassy Suites Hotel

He enters the stately old hotel fifteen minutes before his eleven o'clock shift. Inside the Pine Street doors he pauses, as he often does, to appreciate the scale of the great lobby. Huge white fluted pillars, their Ionic capitals dripping with golden clusters of grapes, support the ornamented ceiling.

"The gentleman that built the hotel," Mr. Thomas says, "he had a dream." A balcony runs halfway around the room, adorned with a festooned golden M, the original crest of the old Multnomah Hotel. The lobby and upper galleries are lit with art deco chandeliers, heavy rings of bronze with opaque white lenses. The floral carpet is a riot of green, gold, and plum, colors repeated in the massive potted palms, settees, chairs, lamps, and Oriental screens. All of this lavishness Mr. Thomas observes with satisfaction.

Crossing the lobby, he greets the night manager and nods to a well-dressed businessman who stands at the front desk. Mr. Thomas is six foot two and dressed in tan slacks and a navy blazer with brass buttons. A light-skinned African American, he has a pleasant and attentive face. He wears tortoiseshell glasses and his tightly cropped hair is receding at the temples. He moves, easy in his body, easy in his uniform, making his way to a heavy desk of polished dark wood, just past Registration, a desk used during the day by the hotel concierge and exclusively by Mr. Thomas at night.

He reads the log entries from the previous shift to see if there's any situation he needs to be aware of, and then he begins his rounds of the hotel, a task he will perform four times during the night. He starts at the top; he takes the elevator to the eighth floor and walks every corridor, on the alert for irregularities.

"On the guest floors, if a door's open that's bad news. I call down to the front desk and ask them if that room is occupied. And if they get back to me and say, 'Yes, it is,' instead of closing the door myself and scaring the life out of the guest, I'll have the front desk phone and tell the guest his door's propped open.

"There are transients who know the ins and outs of the hotel," Mr. Thomas observes. "If one of them comes to the lobby and slips by you, and gets up on the floor and finds a room or a door open, he's going to spend the night royally."

Mr. Thomas takes the stairs down to the seventh floor and repeats the process. After he's checked all the guest floors, he goes back downstairs and records all of this in his log, where he'll make an entry every hour on the hour.

When he's not on his rounds, he positions himself in the lobby. "That way, there's always somebody at that front desk who's got an extra pair of eyes, an extra pair of ears. We also have cameras, which are a big help to us. They'll capture anybody walking out with something, or trying to get in."

He feels a distinct affection for his gaudy surroundings, often marveling that he, Erik Thomas, has taken such an unlikely route to this city, this historic hotel. And he feels, at sixty-two, that he has come to the last job he will ever have.

From Ohio he came originally, one of four who survived in a family of six children. His was one of maybe six hundred black families in Piqua, Ohio, then a town of twenty-two thousand people.

"My father had some people in Kentucky and they lived in the back woods. They all lived in proximity, maybe a mile from one another, in a kind of valley. They didn't have any electric and no phones. They were poor." His most indelible childhood impression is from a trip his father took him on when he was five years old.

"There were two older ladies lived together. They wore long cotton dresses with aprons, bandannas, earrings. And they were black, blacker than coal. One smoked a corncob pipe, and the other would be spitting chewing tobacco into the can, and I just thought that was really something. I used to sit there on the porch and study them.

"In the evening time somebody would strike up a song, and he would tell the story of his day, the whole story of his day in song. It was really something: you could hear them a mile away. And then the next night, somebody else would tell the whole story of their day. I remember it because it was so beautiful, especially the songs. Can you imagine somebody putting their whole day in a song?"

For more than half a century, Mr. Thomas has marveled over the existence of that isolated community, transplanted whole from another world. Today, he is still attracted to African culture. Some day, he has even thought, he will travel to that vast continent and visit the great Serengeti Plain.

A year after his trip to Kentucky, another childhood experience changed his life: he saw his first horse.

"I saw them up above there, riding along the levee, two white men on horseback. I followed them. They were riding out toward the dam, and I took a short cut and caught up with them. When the older man saw me, he turned around in his saddle and said, 'What is your name, boy?'

"'Erik Thomas,' I said.

"'Bud Thomas's boy?' he asked.

"And when I said yes, he picked me up and put me on the saddle in front of him. It was Mr. Frank McCullough, and he was out riding with his son. He taught me everything I know about horses. I loved that man."

When he was old enough, he got a job at a riding stable. He started working with quarter horses and Appaloosa, and turned professional when he was twenty-one. "And then I had an urge to go to California. I knew there was something there."

In Walnut Creek, he managed to get hired at John Rogers Arabians, a top-notch breeding stable and home of the legendary stallion, Serafix, who would sire more than thirty national winners.

"When I saw Serafix I was really taken aback. He was at least sixteen-and-a-half hands! The Arabians that I had seen back east were Egyptian-bred horses and they were very small, fifteen hands. I didn't ride them, because my feet dragged the ground. This horse was a breeding stallion, a beautiful animal, chestnut. He got all his awards—top ten halter horse, top ten pleasure horse: he was phenomenal. People sent Mr. Rogers their mares from all over the country."

For Mr. Thomas, *The Man from Snowy River*, an Australian film made in 1982, is the best introduction to the work he did training horses in the ring. In the film, the young mountain man, John, breaks work horses; Mr. Thomas broke horses for show.

"You ever see how that boy works with that horse?" he says of the film. "I always bitted my horses up before I put the saddle on them. Just let them get used to it. Then introduce them to the loosened saddle, and then tighten up just a little bit, not too much. Let them buck; let them buck again. Actually, I only had one horse do that. I've trained many horses; I've only had one horse buck. Then you start them out on leads—walk, trot, canter. It's all there in the movie. I always liked my stallions half crazy. That gets the judge's attention."

He was on his way to show horses in Canada when he first saw Oregon, and he found the countryside beautiful. Then an Oregon breeder brought him up to qualify a stallion and a filly for the Grand Nationals, and Mr. Thomas worked out of the man's stable in Wilsonville.

"But I found Oregon a little bit different than California. Money is no object there; people spend money. I worked hard getting those two horses ready for the Grand Nationals, but then the owner said, 'We just don't have the money to send them there.' That really kind of broke my heart, because I put a lot of time and effort in, and he never even sent them to show."

For a while Mr. Thomas taught equestrianship at a public stable in Tualatin, then opened his own stable, east of Portland, with twelve horses.

"I had gotten an itch to go back into training. A woman came to me with a pinto. I was busy with Arabians and didn't want to be bothered, but I did finally take him on, and I won every class I showed him in; he was unbeatable in Oregon. He won his Legion of Honor, but, here again, she didn't have the means to send him to the nationals. I thought, What's the use? I kind of hung it up after that."

After the guest rooms, Mr. Thomas checks the lower level, where there's a tiled room with swimming pool and sauna, and a separate exercise room. He continues on to the basement where the Arcadian Room once had seating sufficient for six hundred at dinner and a stage large enough for a full orchestra. For years, the famous free Sunday night concerts were broadcast over Radio KXL from this room at the old Multnomah Hotel.

There are not a lot of guests about at this hour, but Mr. Thomas is always interested in chatting with anyone who happens to be still up.

"I've met some people who've been coming to the hotel for years, and it's fascinating. I like to listen to them because they can point out things to me that I didn't know. I spoke with one woman whose mother got married here, and she herself got married here, and she's probably in her sixties or seventies. And now her daughter was recently married at the hotel, so it's a family tradition." Mr. Thomas, who has been in town for a little more than twenty years, feels like a newcomer.

In Portland, once he got out of training horses, he had to decide how to make a living. He was forty-three years old and he'd never known anything but horses. For more than twenty years, he had held the opinion that working with animals was a little better than working with people.

Then a friend who was director of security at Emanuel Hospital approached Mr. Thomas about going to work with him. "Most of the security officers that I had seen were overweight, with big stomachs hanging over their duty belts and run-over shoes. I said, 'No.'"

But when he visited, he found it wasn't like that. "I saw nice clean uniforms, so I said, 'Sure.'"

He worked a day shift at Emanuel for five years, until the hospital began putting their resources into building the new trauma center, and Mr. Thomas noted they were laying off nurses. "I knew that security and housekeeping were the next to go." So he took a couple of weeks off, then called a friend who had offered a job at the Fred Meyer chain of stores. "I worked at Interstate Fred Meyer, I worked at Peninsula Fred Meyer, I worked at them all."

In 1991, he was offered more money by Lloyd Center, an urban shopping mall, for work that was part security and part public relations. Working sometimes days, sometimes swing, Mr. Thomas had lots of interaction with the security officers hired by the individual stores, and their limited conversation began to wear on him. "Everybody's got a story to tell: how they caught this or that person. Everybody had the *same* story. I knew I was going to switch jobs."

He began actively looking at the same time that Promus Corporation began advertising. He was hired before the Multnomah Hotel renovation was completed, and was on the job at the time of the hotel's grand opening. In some ways, he feels he is back keeping the company he kept when he was training thoroughbreds in California among the rich.

But night shift was a hard transition. "It like to killed me. I was up when I should have been to bed, tired when I came to work. I couldn't even eat. It was August, so we had really long days. I had moved downtown, and the traffic kept me awake. I had never lived in the city before, always in the country. Everything kept me awake." But after some months, he found his rhythm, and began to appreciate the independence and solitude of night shift.

The mezzanine-level banquet rooms must be checked, even though they're dark and empty at this hour. His particular favorite is the Queen Marie, a fifty-six- by forty-foot ballroom with twenty-foot ceilings. Mirrors run along one wall and opposite them tall windows with drapes, floor to ceiling, of plush burgundy with gold stars.

Built to be the showiest in the Pacific Northwest, the Multnomah Hotel originally had 725 rooms. On February 8, 1912, eight thousand guests showed up for the grand opening. Two consecutive owners went bankrupt within the first four years, until Eric Hauser, a shipbuilder from Minnesota, bought it in 1916. For nearly five decades the hotel was operated first by Mr. Hauser and then by his son. During those years, illustrious guests included Theodore Roosevelt, Warren G. Harding, Herbert Hoover, Franklin Delano Roosevelt, President Eisenhower, and the Kennedy brothers on a 1960 spring campaign tour. The stars stayed here—Lana Turner, Joan Crawford, Jimmy Stewart, Bing Crosby, Bob Hope, and Elvis Presley. Col. Charles Lindbergh came in September 1927, halfway through a nine-month national tour. Portland gave a parade in his honor, and the dinner at the Multnomah Hotel was attended by five hundred guests.

Now Mr. Thomas stands in the doorway of the ballroom and flips a switch, illuminating the crystal chandeliers. This room is named for Queen Marie of Romania, who visited in 1926 at the invitation of railroad baron Sam Hill. Officially, Hill had asked her to dedicate Maryhill, the formal mansion he was building on the Columbia River; unofficially, Hill hoped she'd leave her husband (she wouldn't). Mr. Thomas likes to imagine the elegance of that era, the swoosh of ballgowns following the first notes of the violins.

The lights went off all over the hotel in 1965, when the General Services Administration remodeled the building as offices for the U.S. Forest Service and Internal Revenue Service. They ripped out rooms and historic detailing, dropped ceilings, and installed fluorescent lights and poorly engineered heating and ventilation systems. When the federal offices moved out, in 1991, the hotel sat empty for four years until two investors bought it for $1.4 million. Two years later the restoration was completed, the original 725 rooms had been reduced to 276, and $35 million had been spent. Just before the opening, the hotel was sold to Promus Hotel Corporation, of Memphis, Tennessee.

Next on Mr. Thomas's rounds is the exterior of the building. "I just walk around the building and see if everything's fine, okay, if the lights are on, no hazardous materials lying on the sidewalk."

The hotel owns the parking garage across the street, and Mr. Thomas takes pride in the fact that the hotel keeps it patrolled. "A lot of the garages in this neighborhood have been having problems with theft, cars and stuff taken out of cars. I think the reason we don't have them in our garage is simply because of the fact that it's well-lit."

Each time Mr. Thomas makes the exterior tour, the scene downtown has changed. "From 11:00 to 2:30 in the morning, if it's not the nightclubs it's the kids cruising in cars. In this area you've got Callahan's open until 2:30, and Portland Steak and Chophouse has a bar, though that closes at 11:00—Lord ask why! They could stay open." The Chophouse is the restaurant off the hotel lobby, a richly paneled room with a gentlemen's club atmosphere and a second entrance from SW 3rd Avenue.

"But after that, the only thing that's on the street is City trucks and street sweepers. At three it's peace and quiet. The only *people* that you find out are the walkers, people who walk through the neighborhood all night long. Some of them are selling drugs. Some are people who can't sleep."

After Mr. Thomas has completed his inspection of the outside, he returns to his desk and makes an entry in his log. When not making his rounds, Mr. Thomas stays at this desk. "The guests can call me, but nine times out of ten they'll call the front desk and say, 'I'm having a problem.' And the front desk will call me.

"After eleven—that's when engineering goes home, that's when housekeeping leaves—after eleven I become engineering, housekeeping and security. I work in the food service if they're busy or swamped, taking trays up to rooms."

His favorite part of the job he saves for last: "I go upstairs to the roof and make sure everything is all right, make sure there are no stow-ins up there." This roof, which is the size of a city block, also played a part in Portland history: a biplane was launched here, carrying letters across the Columbia River to Vancouver, in the early days of air mail delivery service.

"I check the machinery, make sure the air conditioning is okay. After that's done, I just stand there and marvel out at the city. It's so beautiful at 3:00, 3:30 in the morning."

To the west stands the U.S. Bank Tower, a pink monolith that Mr. Thomas doesn't much care for, and behind that, the graceful sweep of the Fremont Bridge. To the west, between Mr. Thomas and the river, is the Market Street Theater, a small turn-of-the-century building ornamented like a wedding cake, much more to Mr. Thomas's taste.

He stands there in the darkness, admiring the bridges, necklaces of lights strung across the water, and contemplating the stately silhouettes of buildings that line the shore. From his post on the roof, Mr. Thomas is an unseen observer of the city's night beauty, but also a listener. Far across the rooftops he imagines a song starting up, perhaps a mile off, yet audible to him in the stillness, a song of this particular city and the passing of another day.

Up All Night

Nightly Bread

Eighteen thousand pounds of sponges are waiting for Dan Kelner when he goes on shift at 10:00 p.m. They're waiting in the sponge fermentation room, in thirteen big rolling iron bins called trolls, where they are growing larger by the minute. Though he mixed none of them himself, these sponges are what Dan will use to make his first several thousand packages of buns each night.

"So if the guy ahead of me made a mistake, it's already made," says Dan, with his characteristic easy smile. "And then it's my baby."

Short and stocky, with a ruddy, hospitable face, Dan Kelner, fifty-six, is the graveyard-shift bun mixer at Franz Bakery. At work, his grey, flyaway hair, beginning to bald in two high widow's peaks, is tucked into a regulation white hairnet. Like the rest of the bakery crew, Dan dresses in whites.

Dan is working from a computer-generated order sheet, which he consults when he first comes on shift. Working alone upstairs in the mixing room, Dan sets in motion the entire automated baking operation, based on the numbers on this sheet and on any handwritten notes from the bun-line foreman, Jeff Otterson.

"If he wants me to add water or subtract water, he'll write a notation on the sheet and then I'll do it. But he's really the only guy I have to answer to other than the guys I relieve and, like I say, I just hope that their sponges are right." (In the mixing room, it's a *sponge* before the first rising, and *dough* after it's risen and has salt and sugar.)

The order sheet tells Dan how many of which products he'll mix tonight, specialty buns for Burgerville, Burger King, Arby's, Carl Jr's, Jack-in-the-Box, and Wendy's, along with the hot dog and hamburger buns sold in grocery stores under the Franz brand label. Tonight, the largest single order is 105,300 four-inch yellow buns for Wendy's.

"We call them formulas rather than recipes," Dan says. "Wendy's got a different formula, Burger King's got a different formula, Burgerville's got a different formula. They like to have their own formulas to say, 'This is *our* product,' but basically they're all pretty much the same."

All of the formulas are based on one hundred pounds of flour, which generally means fifty pounds of water. "You set a dial as to how much flour you want to go into your hopper, which is right above the mixing machine. Like if you want 230 pounds, you set 230, and then you just push a button and it pumps in 230 pounds."

Flour is delivered every two days and it's stored, along with the other ingredients, on the first floor. From here, the flour is pushed through a shaking box to be sifted and then piped two flights upstairs, at thirty pounds per second, to two cylindrical tanks, each holding one hundred and fifty thousand pounds of flour. From these tanks it is piped to Dan, as he needs it to mix buns, and likewise to the mixer on the bread side.

To the flour, Dan adds water and yeast and any other ingredients except sugar and salt. He turns on the mixing machine, a huge metal cylinder with mixer bars running through the center, that whirls and beats the sponge. By pushing a button, he lowers the front metal door and sets the cylinder rocking, and this "kicks" the huge sponge out into a waiting dough troll, an iron bin that looks like a dumpster without a lid. He rolls the troll across the brick floor into the sponge fermentation room, where the sponge will sit for four hours and rise three feet.

Next, he rolls the troll with the largest sponge, the one that's already been waiting the full four hours, out of the fermentation room and onto the troll hoist, which lifts it up high enough to rock the inflated sponge into the mixer again. He adds 14 pounds of salt and 136 pounds of sugar—with some variation for formula—and pushes a button to close the door. After it's mixed, a matter of seven minutes, Dan lowers the front metal door and kicks fifteen hundred pounds of dough back out into the troll, then rolls it across the scales.

"The reason to weigh it is because sometimes you might leave an ingredient out. Guys sometimes might leave the sugar out. If it's like anywhere from twenty to eighty pounds light, you're going, 'Wait a minute. How come this dough is light?' So a lot of times you catch it by weighing it on the scale. Then you got to bring it back and throw it back into the mixer and add it."

Since this rarely happens, the troll is generally rolled off the scales, out through the mixer room door, and onto a big steel platform above the bun line. Here Dan dumps the new dough down a chute to the bun-making operation.

Directly below is the KRD machine, the machine that cuts the dough. "They just call it the Model K," Dan explains. "It's incredible. It takes the bread dough and forms it to the kind of bun that you're going to be making at the time—a hot dog or a hamburger bun—and puts it in the pans, and the dough goes on its way."

In the bun mixing room, Dan continues to make fresh sponges, and to add salt and sugar to those sponges which have already had a chance to rise. The job has a predictable rhythm, though the weather adds a note of unpredictability. Since the building is not heat-regulated—it has neither heating nor air conditioning—the sponge fermentation room can range from 85 to 110 degrees, depending on the season.

"You go by the weather. You got ice water to adjust the internal temperature of the sponge. You can make it cooler to compensate for being so hot in that room so that by the time it does come around, it's the temperature that it should be."

Dan alternates between mixing sponges and kicking out doughs until it's time for his break.

Meanwhile, down below, after the dough has been cut into buns, it is dropped into trays of twenty-four, which are moving all the time. For fifty-five minutes they are slowly conveyed through the proof box, a big room kept at 105 degrees, where the dough rises again. (An old joke told in the bakery is that in the summer it's so hot out there on the floor, that you go in the proof box to get cool.)

Still moving, the buns are sprayed with water, and sesame seeds are sprinkled on them. They spend eight minutes baking; at any given time, forty-two hundred hot dog buns are moving through the oven. Four levels of conveyor belts move buns around overhead as they cool. Below, crumbs are swept up, collected in six-hundred-pound bins, and sold at one cent per pound to hog farmers for feed.

After the buns cool, they're sliced, packaged, and racked. These racks roll down a moving ramp called an "alligator" onto trucks headed for Shasta, Eureka, and Yreka, to the south, and to Longview and Vancouver to the north. Eastbound trucks head out the Columbia River Gorge. Checkers load the bread trucks twenty-four hours a day, a fleet of thirty-two semis, yellow with the blue Franz oval, and another 320 route trucks, including those designated with the Pierre's or Archway logo.

Franz is the largest independently owned, family-held bakery in the country, and the businesses that it has absorbed chronicle the demise of the small family bakery in the Pacific Northwest—Pierre's in Portland, Archway Cookies in McMinnville, Gai's in Seattle, Williams in Eugene, and Snyder's in Tacoma.

Today the original bakery built by the Franz brothers in 1912, at NE 11th and Flanders, is a Portland landmark, for the seven-layer maze of conveyor belts that can be glimpsed by motorists through the long windows on 12th Avenue, for the huge red and white loaf of bread that revolves atop the building, and for the bakery fragrance that fills the neighborhood for blocks.

"Of all the jobs in this bakery, I think mixing is the best," Dan says. "It all starts there! I mean, if that's wrong, then the whole operation is wrong. I take pride in my work, I'm good at what I do, the time goes by fast. I just enjoy it. I wouldn't want to have any other job in the bakery."

▲

Dan Kelner was raised in Portland, where his father drove for Wonder Bread for twenty-five years. "I had some kind of little rinky-dink jobs—I worked up at Mt. Hood at the ski lodge, I worked down at Meier & Frank for about a year." He graduated from Central Catholic in 1961 and worked for two years for the Porter-Scarpelli Macaroni Company, then on NE 35th and Broadway, which made spaghetti. After two years in the Army, stationed in Santo Domingo, and marriage to Judy, his high-school sweetheart, Dan went back to work for Porter-Scarpelli.

"The old man that owned it, I'll never forget one time when I was working graveyard shift, and he came in. It was a Sunday morning, and it was just me and I was cleaning up. He always came in in the morning, and he would sit on his table and he'd dangle his feet over the edge. He was about ninety-one years old at the time. And he said, 'How are things going?' And I said, 'Oh, they're going real good, Sam.' I said, 'We really had a good night last night.' And I go, 'How are you doing?' He says, 'You know, I was just lying in bed last night and I was praying to God if He'd just give me ten more years, I think I could really get this place going.' He's ninety-one years old, now, and he just wanted ten more years from God! To get that thing just the way he wanted. But he was quite an old man, quite the guy.

"The place was a goldmine. There was probably thirty employees, and they were the only spaghetti factory in the state of Oregon. The old man, he was ninety-three years old when he finally died. Anyway, I worked there for fifteen years.

"When they closed down the macaroni factory, the union recommended, 'Look, if you guys are smart, don't even go to apply at a bakery because they work those guys to death. Those guys kill themselves in the summertime, their hours are crappy, and it's just terrible work.' They were talking about the heat and the heat exhaustion at a bread bakery. They recommended places like Frito-Lay and Nabisco.

"So the first thing I did was try a bakery. Here I am, I got a wife and a two-year-old son, and I'm out of work for the first time in my life, so I'm kind of in a panic. Anyway, I went down to Franz Bakery and applied, and when the guy called me he said, 'I got an application here for you.' I said, 'Yeah?' And he said, 'I see on here that you worked for Porters for fifteen years, and you missed one day.' And I said, 'Yeah.' And he said, 'What did you miss that day for?' And I said, 'I can't even remember, but it was probably a funeral. That would have been the only time I would have missed a day.' And the guy said, 'Can you come to work?' So I went to work there, and I've been working there ever since." That was in 1977.

▲

His break over, Dan climbs the stairs to the mixing room and resumes making sponges.

"I like the solitude working up here in the mixing room. Whenever they have tours or inspections, that usually goes on in the daytime. I'm not particularly crazy about that kind of stuff. I mean I got enough to worry about doing my job right.

"But if I've got any problems, I'm all by myself. I've got to get some help in here, and I've got to get it right now, cause this stuff is something that can't wait. My foreman can get here probably in a couple of minutes. When I call him he drops whatever he's doing and he'll come up right away. Because he knows that if I'm down, everybody's down. I stop, everybody stops. And they're paying everybody to just stand there and wait for me. But I very seldom ever call him 'cause I very seldom ever have a problem."

More commonly, if something goes wrong the trouble's down below. "For instance, if something got caught in the KRD [dough cutting machine]. Things like that happen, where guys'll throw an oven mitt on the ground or something, it'll get in a pan and they'll go to throw that pan back and not notice the oven mitt. The oven mitt will go down inside the KRD, and you're down! They've got to tear everything apart. When that machine is down, I'm down, 'cause I got no place to put my dough.

"A real bad night would be if the electricity went out. Power failure. Usually in the wintertime somebody'll hit a power pole or lightning strikes a power line. That's happened, where the whole bakery's gone dead. I mean black! Pitch black, where you can't even see your hand. And you got all this stuff ready to be made up …

"You just wait for the power company to fix it, and then when it comes back on, you know that there's going to be trouble. Things don't kick back on, and then they've got to reset everything. They've had times where they've been down for three or four hours, and that the stuff coming out by this time is just rotten. It just sits there and in the meantime all that yeast is cooking, and by the time it comes out it's just jello.

"They've got engineers here twenty-four hours a day, at least three on every shift. If you got any problems with a machine, you're not supposed to touch it—the engineers are up here right now. A good night is if everything runs fine and you never have to call an engineer. I've had good nights like that, where nobody talks on that intercom." But those are few and far between at Franz, because there are 150 different kinds of machines, between the bread and the bun side.

"I'd say where I have probably the most problems would be the rubber seal in the front of the mixer that keeps the water from running out the door. If that seal breaks—sometimes it gets a hole in it or blows out—I got water leaking all over the place.

"But it's a nice place to work. I've had guys that work on scales—they come in every six months and make sure that everything's weighing right—I've had more guys tell me what a fantastic place this is, how clean it is. And it is: they spend a lot of money every year, keeping the place looking good. It's a first class operation."

Dan has tried the other shifts and has always gone back to nights. "I've always been a night person, even when I was young. I'm one of those kind of guys who could stay up till four or five o'clock in the morning and I don't have any problem. A lot of people can't work graveyard shift. They come to work at the bakery, and they're down here three or four days and they go, 'I'm going to lose my mind.'

"I like those kind of hours. On my day off, I'll lay down for maybe two or three hours in the morning and then get up and stay up for the rest of the day. Usually I don't go to bed till probably three or four o'clock. I watch television or I go downstairs and listen to my music and watch my fish—I've got an aquarium downstairs. The time goes by so fast. Here it's four o'clock in the morning, I haven't been to sleep yet.

"A lot of times I come up and just go sit out on the back porch, three or four in the morning, grab a beer and just sit out there with the dog and look around. I don't know why I'm sitting there, but I enjoy doing stuff like that. I do like the night a lot."

When Dan leaves the bakery in the morning, he likes to come straight home and sit in the kitchen with Judy. "I've got to tell her everything that goes on. 'Did anything exciting happen?' The guys down there, she knows them all, and there's always something to tell about somebody.

"'Well, what happened to so-and-so?' she'll ask.

"And I got to fill her in on all that stuff before I'm allowed to read my newspaper. If I come home and I go, 'Nothing happened, honey, nothing happened today.' 'Well, something had to happen! You can't tell me you're down there for eight hours and nobody told you anything!'

"She just amazes me. I've been with her for, God, like thirty-four or thirty-five years. We met when I was seventeen and she was fifteen. A lot of women can't take these kind of hours. They really can't. But Judy's never had a problem. She's always been, 'Hey, that's your job, that's the way you do, and we got to make the best of it.'

"Judy's got a little bread machine and she puts in her mixes and it grinds it up and cooks it right in there. I don't make bread at all. That's the way it is, it's like a carpenter: does he ever do any work around his house? No! But give me two hundred pounds of water and four hundred pounds of flour, I'll make a heck of a loaf of bread."

Up All Night

Flowers for the City

Tuesday night around midnight the driver of a forty-eight-foot semi takes I-5's Going Street exit and heads west to Swan Island, an industrial basin on the Willamette River's east shore. He crosses a viaduct over the Union Pacific tracks, then pulls into the rear of the Portland Flower Market, a concrete building longer than a city block. He backs the semi up against the loading dock, right by the door to Frank Adams Wholesale Florist. He has the key to their big walk-in cooler: it's here he will unload.

The driver begins to wheel in his freight, stacking it on pallets. He's come all the way from San Diego, picking up product along the way—delphinium and Queen Anne's lace from Oxnard, gladiolas from Santa Maria, orchids and lilies from Arcata. Other boxes are stamped Ventura, Carpinteria, Nopomo, Watsonville. There are asparagus plumosus and tree fern from San Antonio, leatherleaf from an old town on the shores of Lake Catemaco, deep in the Veracruz jungle, and protea all the way from New Zealand.

When he finishes, the driver has stacked sixty-six boxes on four pallets. He studies the manifest once again: it reads sixty-eight. He counts one more time, carefully. Nope, only sixty-six. He makes a note of the shortage on the manifest, initials it, and leaves it beneath another sign: **TRUCKERS Please Put Bills in This Box**. He leaves the cooler and locks the door behind him. He's still got to drive to Seattle tonight, another hundred and eighty miles.

▲

At 2:30 in the morning, Jeffrey Peck, operations manager for Frank Adams Wholesale Florist, turns off his bedside alarm. "I have to say when that alarm goes off, I'm up, I'm happy, I'm in my routine."

With sandy hair and a medium build, Jeffrey, at thirty-two, is the boy next door, personable and clean-cut. In the morning he has an unvarying routine. "I like to futz around and get things going," he says agreeably. "I'm definitely a morning person." He showers and shaves at his leisure, then leaves for work at 3:45.

He unlocks at Frank Adams at four o'clock, and turns on all the lights in the vast warehouse. The entire flower market—a convenient string of neighboring related businesses—comprises one hundred ten thousand square feet, of which Frank Adams, the largest of the wholesalers, uses thirty thousand.

The first thing Jeffrey does is check the cooler to make sure the California truck arrived last night.

Although the business doesn't open to the retail florists until 6:00 a.m., there is a lot to be done now, and another nine staff people arrive at 4:30 to help do it—one cut-flower buyer, five salespeople, and three delivery drivers, needed early to help get the orders on the truck they'll drive that day.

"The first thing is to get everybody organized," Jeffrey says. "Kind of get a game plan on what you're going to be doing, what truck needs to be out earliest, what product's going, pulling standing orders for weddings or parties or whatever. That is top priority, that we pull those orders before we open our main door for general business.

"So, make sure the orders *are* being pulled. Make sure that our buyer is bringing in good product, and if the product's bad, making sure that we get credit on the product." The short delivery is not a problem: the truck driver's calculation will stand, and Frank Adams will be credited for the two missing boxes.

In cold storage, the salespeople check their orders against the new boxes and cut the tight plastic straps. They have designated racks in the cooler where they can store whatever flowers they need for special orders coming up during the week. This way, the product doesn't get moved out to the floor and sold.

"Monday, Wednesday, and Friday—from back in the forties, they're considered market days," Jeffrey explains. "A good chunk of the retailers come in here to pick out their flowers on those days. We're hauling everything out of the coolers and putting it out here on the floor for people to shop, 'cause they don't like going into the coolers to do the shopping. And we're really pressed to get it all done from before six, when we open the doors."

Using a yard-long pole with a hook, the crew steers dollies, racks, and big tubs of flowers along the concrete floor, like children pulling wagons. They weave in and out without saying much, building an indoor garden beneath the high fluorescent lights. Soft rock music wafts from the cut-flower buyer's radio, turned low.

By 5:30, the air is fragrant with all these flowers, though Jeffrey, like many of the other people who work here, admits to not noticing many of the perfumes anymore. Mostly it's just the fragrant tuberoses and the well-named chocolate cosmos that still get his attention.

"Stock has a really clean, real natural kind of scent to it," he points out. "It's one of those that's really nice when you get it in, but the stems on the stock take on a horrible smell after about two days in a bucket. To where everybody says, 'Oh, who just dumped the stock bucket?' That's just a standing joke. The product's still good, but the water itself, you can smell it across the store."

Just before the doors open, the floor is gaudy with color. There's flax and heather, which came on the California truck, and cornflowers of the brightest blue. Huge bunches of orange, yellow, and pink alstroemeria, wrapped in cellophane sleeves, sit in front of the drooping burgundy tassels of amaranthus. Electric blue hydrangeas contrast with hefty golden sunflowers and dramatic fan-like birds of paradise, which arrive by Federal Express, along with the other "tropicals" from Hawaii.

A few minutes before the doors open for business, the standing orders arrive from the Oregon Flower Growers Association next door—delphinium, zinnias, and potted plants. This morning they've delivered seven colors of dahlias, which are set out in buckets right near the entrance—burgundy, candy stripe, tangerine, yellow, orchid, blood red, and watermelon.

"Once in a while," Jeffrey admits, "I sometimes just go, Wow!"

Precisely at six, the retail florists are admitted to roam among the displays, some braving the front cooler. (They're not allowed in the back cooler, where the special orders are carefully guarded.) There are older women in kimonos or slacks, and younger women in skirts or shorts; older men in sports coats and younger men in tight-fitting jeans. Some wheel shopping carts and some carry armloads of flowers. All wear white plastic buyers' badges and all are pretty much in a hurry.

In the wholesale business, new people are usually first brought on as drivers. "We start training them immediately on product, good product versus bad, this is a rose, this is a carnation," Jeffrey says, "because some people couldn't tell you the difference between a mini-carnation and a regular carnation, between leatherleaf and tree fern. Once the salespeople trust them, we let them pull an order."

Lisa is the top-dollar salesperson, and this morning Jeffrey has assigned all three drivers to help her pull her orders. This is the fourth wholesaler Lisa has worked for; some of her customers have been with her for sixteen or seventeen years.

"I'll tell you flat out," Jeffrey says, "Lisa this month did about $102,000, just in cut flowers, not including supplies. Our next salesperson did $52,000, so Lisa has a full plate."

Lisa is a short, energetic figure in blue jeans and black t-shirt, with curly auburn hair and a phone at one ear. As she talks, she makes lists on torn half-sheets of white paper. "I've got liatris," she says to her customer. "Why don't you try a ten-pack of Mexican leather?" Just before she hangs up, she asks, "If I find something really fun can I throw it on?"

As she scribbles and talks, the drivers pull orders for her, filling her table and nearby buckets with tulips, roses, yellow yarrow, freesia, curly willow, and four-inch Gerber daisies in pink, yellow, and red. The cut-off for the early truck is nine o'clock, and eleven o'clock for the afternoon truck, so mornings are hectic.

Lisa's work space consists of a high counter with her computer and phone, a low worktable with a shelf holding large sheets of waxed paper and newspaper, and a barstool, though she's always too busy to sit. Jeffrey stationed her apart from the other sellers, thinking the segregation would be helpful given her workload, but walk-in customers exit the cooler right into Lisa's space. Just now a heavy-set dishwater-blonde woman emerges from the cooler with a big smile and an armful of white gladiolas. Lisa greets her just as a page comes over the loudspeaker: "Lisa, line 6, please. Lisa, line 6."

She hands a driver four clear plastic boxes of gardenias and picks up the receiver. "Hi, ya, Sharon!" "Yes, Ma'am, I did." "One purple statice, you got it." "Thank *you*, have a good day."

On a rear worktable, Jeffrey is examining a bunch of white Oriental lilies standing in a tall grey bucket. First he pulls out the stamens one at a time, then cleans rust-colored stains off the white petals, one by one, with a pipe cleaner.

Like everyone else on the cut flower side of Frank Adams, Jeffrey handles flowers. He has also kept one big account which he services. "When I pull product, everybody laughs and says, 'That must be Beaverton Florists because it's all purples.' I like the bright colors. A lot of shops today like whites, the creams, soft yellows, but I want it to be bright. I want it to stand out. There's this rose called Hot Princess. It's an import, and the thing is the most gorgeous hot pink."

Yet his very favorite flower is famously pastel. "Lisianthus, it's very soft," Jeffrey says. "It almost looks like a rose with just very few petals. It's got the shape of a rose. And it always reminds me—and this will sound weird—of a pin Grandma used to have. She wore a flower pin in her hair all the time. I didn't know what that was until I went to work and found out it was lisianthus."

It's 6:57 a.m. and the rest of the staff, those who didn't arrive until 6:00, are at work now, too. The manager, Richard Bierman, who has an office on the second floor, is downstairs talking to customers and steering flowers around. A big blonde man with greying beard and moustache, Richard has twenty-seven years in the business. And although he's been in Portland for only the last seven, he relishes telling the story of the early days of the Portland Flower Market.

"The market actually started in 1941, during World War Two. It was Joseph Peterkort, Sr., Bob Hastings, a gentleman by the name of Earl Oliver, and a Mr. Hungerford. They were a bunch of independent growers who decided to have a place where the retailers could shop. Before that, the growers used to go right to all the large retailers and deliver stuff to them. So they started the Portland Flower Market, where all the growers had space.

"Back in the old days, it wasn't real kosher for a grower to have a wholesale house. They were just supposed to be growers and sell what they grew. But Joe Peterkort, Sr., got in with a gentleman by the name of Frank Adams and decided to open a wholesale house. Peterkort actually was a big owner from Day One, but it was never publicized, at all. Everybody thought that Frank Adams owned it all, but he didn't. When he retired, the Peterkorts just bought him out.

"They moved over here from Grand Avenue eight years ago. Oregon Flower Growers Association is the new name for the [original] group of growers, which is a co-op." The Swan Island building is owned by the Growers Association, Frank Adams, and Greenleaf, and together they lease space to USA Floral, which has a bouquet operation, and Billingsley, another wholesaler. As the largest owner at Portland Flower Market, the Frank Adams business helps establish policy and procedures as to who is permitted to buy wholesale.

"We're really trying to make it a little tougher for people to get in here," Richard admits. "We ask at point of sale for the buyer's pass. We turn a lot of people away and make them go and get their pass. There's two types of passes they can have: one is to buy fresh flowers, and in order to do that, they have to have an Oregon Nurseryman's license, and a business license, and to prove that they are in the business to sell these flowers.

"The supply side is a little bit different," he explains. "You don't have to have the nurseryman's license, but you can't buy fresh flowers, only the supplies.' That is, the containers and tools indispensable to florists—tape, ribbon, scissors, knives, floral foam, and so forth. In addition, there are long aisles of silk flowers, Hanukkah wrapping paper, sea chests, bird cages, galvanized buckets and rattan boxes, bells, ruffles, lady bugs, goblets, sleighs, crystal reindeer, ornamental eggs (including a bejewelled egg the size of a backpack), dalmatian dogs, raffia, leprechauns, parrots, blue metallic frogs, lighthouses, wooden cherries, and golden fish.

"All the stuff that's manufactured in China, you're buying a year in advance," Richard points out. "Christmas never ends for us."

Nor is it only the supplies that come halfway around the world. "Domestic growers are throwing away their equipment," he says. "Almost all the production now is being done in South America. Rose production, they have about 70 percent of the market in the U.S. now. Pom poms is about 70 percent, carnations is probably closer to 90 percent.

"Most South American product comes in to Miami, leaves out of there on our refrigerated truck on Wednesday, gets here Saturday. We process it and put it in water on Sunday and then it's ready for customers to buy on Monday."

This development has made it necessary to improve the staying power of flowers. "They've hybridized so much that they're getting some really good shelf life," says Richard. "A big part also is the care and healing of the product. Ethylene is a very big factor in the deterioration of fresh flowers. Flowers produce ethylene just in their natural state of developing. So they have these ethylene blocks they put in the trailers, to keep the ethylene down. They're a pad-type product that hangs in the trucks and *absorbs* ethylene, so it doesn't circulate back into the product."

Richard, who originally planned to be an architect, feels he's "less straitlaced" than the typical CEO. He started out "chopping flowers and putting them in water" when he dropped out of classes at Kansas University. From there he went to sales and then to management.

"I like the people," Mr. Bierman says. "I always tell people that if you tried other things and didn't really fit in, you might like the flower business. I don't think anybody came into this business to be in the business: they all ended up here. And they're all a little bit off the wall. Though you can't stereotype anybody, 'cause we've got all types. Customer-wise, you're dealing with a lot of very creative people."

Jeffrey, whom Mr. Bierman is grooming for management, would take that one step further. "If you are one bit homophobic, you will last about two seconds in the floral business. If you've got hangups about that, this is the wrong industry."

Jeffrey, who was born and raised in Los Angeles, moved to Colorado to go to community college and ended up working for the Department of

Corrections. "I did my internship in a jail at Canyon City and then I went immediately into parole." In 1993, at age twenty-five, he moved to Portland.

"I wanted to be back on the West Coast. I missed being close to the ocean, but I did not want to live back in L.A. I came out here, actually, with no job, thinking to get back into corrections." In the meantime, he went to work for Greenleaf Wholesale Florists.

"I kind of liked the business," he says. "And there's a saying, Once you're in this business for five years, you're stuck." Jeffrey stayed six years with Greenleaf, until a change of management had him "butting heads." He quit.

"It wasn't two days that I had left Greenleaf that there was a message from Richard on my home phone: 'Jeffrey? Richard. Call me.'"

In early 2000, Jeffrey moved over to Frank Adams.

Now that Richard has Jeffrey downstairs as operations manager, and his own wife, Patty, upstairs as office manager, he's found more time to work building a consortium of independent wholesalers, with the hope of getting better buying power abroad.

Downstairs, on the cut-flower floor, it's Jeffrey who handles the emergencies. "We could all go in there and open that cooler door and, guess what? The truck didn't show up last night with fifty cases of flowers. And they're all laughing at me because they can see I'm getting mad for nothing that I have any control over. I immediately get on the phone with our trucking company, and they have satellites now on the trucks so they can pinpoint where that truck's at and give you, within a half an hour, when it's going to be there.

"It seems to be only during holiday times that it happens," he adds.

In this business, Valentine's Day and Mother's Day are the two heaviest rushes. These are the weeks of roses, not just red and white and pink, but novelty roses, like the peach-colored roses with deep orange rims called Leonides and fragrant lavender roses called Lavande. There is even a rose, Bells of Ireland, that is green.

"We have that week of Valentine's when it never slows down. We could probably get in trouble because nobody takes breaks. We tell 'em, 'Go take a break,' but they don't. You don't get lunches and you're there, sometimes, from three in the morning till eleven at night. And you do not sit down."

Providing it is not a holiday week, and providing it is not May or June, which are heavy months for weddings, Jeffrey generally works a ten-hour day, with half a day on Saturday.

"When I get home, I eat and maybe watch a little TV, have a glass of wine, then I go to bed no later than seven. I get up between 2:30 and 2:45 every day of the week, regardless of if it's my day off or not," he says. "It's a lovely, lovely time of the day."

On Sunday morning, he begins by cleaning the house, and then he does the laundry.

"It will sound weird—my hobby's walking. I love to walk. On Sundays I walk from my house to downtown, and I live at SE 85th and Burnside." He takes his yellow lab, Rio, with him and he takes the Sunday morning paper—it's delivered at 4:45. "I tie my dog up out in front of a restaurant and I go in and have breakfast and I'm home by nine o'clock."

The only other time of the week when Jeffrey gets outdoors may be a few minutes stolen to have a quick cigarette on the loading dock behind Frank Adams.

"Whenever there's a beautiful sunrise, somebody from Greenleaf will come down and tell somebody at Adams to tell everybody to go out back. The next thing you know there's fifty people out on the loading dock watching this gorgeous, gorgeous sunrise."

From Swan Island, they are looking east at rose-tinted cloud furrows hanging over the bluff. "The sun just comes over the top of it, and if the clouds are all pink, and the next thing you know the whole market's out there and it's like, 'Who's helping customers?'"

It may be the only time when the staff from all the different competing wholesalers get together. "I'll be honest, there's some people at Greenleaf that I don't …" and Jeffrey trails off without finishing his sentence. "But it's weird, if we're all out there watching that sun come up, I'll look over at the old [Greenleaf] manager, who got hired when I probably should have had the job, and say, 'God, isn't that cool?' and he'll say, 'Yeah, but look at over here!'

"Five minutes later it's over with, and you're back inside hustling around." And coping with a whole new time frame called day.

Up All Night
Acknowledgments

I am grateful to all the people who generously let me tag along behind them as they did their jobs and who took precious time out during the day to answer my myriad questions about their life and work. *Up All Night* is their book, and it has been a privilege to bring their stories to daylight.

In addition to those mentioned by name in the individual chapters, many people made valuable contributions to the book by steering me to a particular worker, easing my access to a job site, or helping me prepare for an interview. In particular, I acknowledge a debt to Dick and Lisa Aanderud, Robert Freedman, Sarah Gies, Debbie Howell, Holly Johnson, Jeff Liddell, Bill Mildenberger, Jack Mulcahy, Kate Nelson, Chris Porter, Mark Schwier, Karl Simon, Jon and Ann Sinclair, and Lacy Turner.

For the individual chapters, I was helped by Julie Ferguson at American Medical Response; Mark Duhrkoop and Julie Stevenson at City Team Ministries; John Hennesey and Ron Springman at Cue's Billiards; Laura Barrett, Jeff Meyers, and Sheila Winsjansen at 800 Support; John Steinbach and Amy Sterrenberg at the Embassy Suites; Sue McAuley, Becky Cartier, Claire Cunningham, Jeff Otterson, and Kevin Sturdy at Franz Bakery; Larry Bauman and Lee Pederson at Jubitz; Greg Gomez at KMHD; Mark Kemball at OHSU; Jane Hartline, Karen Kane, and Cathie Roberts at the Oregon Zoo; Stephanie Oliver at *The Oregonian*; Barbara Craig, Michael Harrison, Randy Johnson, Tim Thrienen, Mary Volm, and Willie Washington at the City of Portland; John Cart, Jan Dabrowski, Chuck Dethloff, and Dale Fenske at Rose City Astronomers; Charlie Geiger at St. Agatha; and Robert Brooks, Harry Hopkins, and Janet Hopper at Tri-Met.

Support for this work was provided by the Regional Arts and Culture Council, which awarded me an encouraging grant at an early and critical phase; Elizabeth Savage, who helped with early research tasks even before the book had begun to take shape; Susan Emmons at Northwest Pilot Project, whose assignments have kept me both fed and inspired; and Melissa Marsland, on whose support, moral, practical, and emotional, I've counted in all my endeavors for the last twenty-six years.

I wish to thank John Becker, Lan Fendors, Jessica Gies, Rosario Hall, and Paula Lifschey for accompanying me on one or more midnight runs; Bobby Weinstock, whose name I always put down as an emergency contact, knowing of his willingness to make a late-night rescue (he never had to); and Jessica Poundstone, Susan Domagalski, Molly Gloss, Mary-Margaret Jenkins, Greta Marchesi, Paul Merchant, Jon Ross, Wayne Scott, and Anna Stone for reading, at various stages, all or part of the manuscript.

Finally, I must thank Jennie Dunham, my agent, who believed in the book despite its setting in faraway Oregon; Mary Elizabeth Braun, who knew she wanted it for OSU Press when she first read it; and her colleagues at the press, Karen Orchard, Jo Alexander, and Tom Booth, always generous with their help.

It was with great satisfaction that I began contacting the principals in this book to tell them that OSU Press planned to publish it, only to have that happiness interrupted with the news that Obdulia Hernandez, who worked so hard as a janitor to support her infant son Oscar, had been killed in a pick-up accident in the Oaxaca countryside on May 2, 2003.

Up All Night has always been dedicated to Marilyn Krueger, without whose friendship and support the book would not have been possible.

Now, under the saddest of circumstances, she shares that dedication with Obdulia's young son, Oscar, whose health and growth and future were his mother's greatest inspiration and concern.